Bipolar Ethics

101 examples of cognitive dissonance
in everyday life

by Roberto De Nicolò

Have you ever noticed how
extraordinary perspective is?
If it didn't exist, you would live in a universe
without a perception of distance
With it however
you can look through many doors
and estimate with a small margin of error
how far you are from the last one

rodenic

Bipolar Ethics

A free study on the habit, shared by almost all human beings, of expressing, at a specific moment in time, a strict and definitive moral judgment against someone considered indisputably guilty of something and deserving of the maximum penalty and all aggravating circumstances, and then behaving exactly like that person in the immediately following moment without any moral qualms and, when accused of inconsistency, applying all mitigating circumstances to oneself.

General index

Definitions

cognitive dissonance "Cognitive dissonance is the state of having inconsistent thoughts, beliefs, or attitudes, especially as relating to behavioral decisions and attitude change. It refers to the mental discomfort experienced by a person who simultaneously holds two or more contradictory beliefs, ideas, or values. This discomfort often leads to an alteration in one of the beliefs, attitudes, or behaviors to reduce the discomfort and restore balance."

[Leon Festinger, A Theory of Cognitive Dissonance, 1957, Stanford Univ. Press]

Ethics (noun) [from Latin ethĭca, Greek ἠϑικά, neuter plural of the adjective ἠϑικός: see ethical]. - In philosophical language, every doctrine or speculative reflection concerning the practical behavior of humans, especially insofar as it intends to indicate what true good is and the means to achieve it, what moral duties are towards oneself and others, and what criteria are used to judge the morality of human actions: Socratic ethics, hedonistic ethics, Kantian ethics, utilitarian ethics, Nietzschean ethics; Nicomachean Ethics and Eudemian Ethics, titles of two moral works by Aristotle. In a broader sense, a complex of moral norms and customs that define specific behavior in relational life with reference to particular historical situations: Greek ethics, Christian ethics; Protestant ethics, which, according to the theories of the German sociologist Max Weber (1864-1920), would have shaped the spirit of capitalism in Europe after the 16th century in Protestant countries, or among Protestant sects within Catholic countries. In particular, professional ethics, the set of duties strictly related to professional activities carried out in society.

[https://www.treccani.it/vocabolario/etica/]

Bipolar (adjective) [compound of *bi-* and *pole*]. – **1.** In a general sense, having two poles, or, figuratively, having two centers, two characteristic and equally important points, or similar: *bipolar political system* (see bipolarism). **2.** With particular technical meanings: **a.** In electrical engineering, of a machine or device that has a single pair of magnetic poles: *bipolar inductor*; or of elements consisting of or related to two conductors: *bipolar plug, bipolar cable, bipolar switch.* **b.** In computer science, *bipolar signals*, in contrast to *unipolar signals*, are signals in which different electrical polarities are used to represent different logical states. **c.** In biology, *bipolar bacteria*, which tend to intensely stain at the poles; *bipolar cells*, nerve cells that have two extensions of approximately the same size. **d.** In medicine, of a pathological condition characterized by oscillating between two opposing elements or symptoms, for example, manic-depressive syndrome.

[https://www.treccani.it/vocabolario/etica/]

Bipolar ethics (noun phrase) – Every doctrine or speculative reflection concerning the practical behavior of humans, indicating alternately what the momentary good and the means to achieve it are, and the momentary evil and the means to achieve it; what the momentary moral duties towards oneself are and what the momentary moral duties towards others are, and what the provisional criteria are to judge the morality of human actions in a pathological condition characterized by oscillating between two (or more) opposing elements. Bipolar ethics is a theory of ethics that is based on two (or more) contrasting or "polar" moral principles. These two (or more) principles are often in conflict and can represent opposite extremes in terms of ethical values without distinction between what is right and what is wrong.

[Title chosen by the author for this book]

Preface

It happens to all of us, multiple times a day. Perhaps some individuals are more susceptible, others less so. You can call it *cognitive dissonance, bipolarity, ethical multipolarity*, or more prosaically, *inconsistency*. However, the phenomenon of being unable to apply a consistent judgment criterion to oneself and others, in the same situations experienced at different times and playing alternate roles, is as common as few other human phenomenologies.

Yet, we rarely grasp the extent of this phenomenon. We are unable to autonomously recognize our unjust partiality in every single expression, decision, evaluation. To acquire this competence, it is necessary for someone else to confront us with the two versions of ourselves.

This book discusses *cognitive dissonance* and the real effects it has on each of our lives, doing so through a series of example episodes chosen as emblematic.

Psychological sciences and definitions

But what do we mean when we talk about *bipolar ethics*? Is there a clear definition that outlines the phenomenon? Before starting to work on this book, I asked my wife to help provide the theoretical foundations and statements that psychological science uses to define the phenomenon.

My kind spouse holds a master's degree in computer science and will soon complete her second degree in psychology. As a dedicated scholar and enthusiast of this discipline, she promptly and effectively responded to my request. Psychology refers to the phenomena described in this book as *cognitive dissonance*. The first to theorize this phenomenon, in 1957, was the American sociologist and psychologist Leon Festinger in his book 'A Theory of Cognitive Dissonance'.

It's a clarifying book on all the psychological processes leading to dissonance, the factors that intensify it, and especially all the practices individuals use to reduce this dissonance. I highly recommend purchasing it.

My book builds on Festinger's remarkable definitions and, without aiming or being able to match its quality, it simply selects, from everyday life, some clearly more frequent and representative cases of the phenomenon, aiming to make it evident and recognizable to the reader who may, in these examples, try to identify a sort of *pattern*.

Leon Festinger, in his book, defined cognitive dissonance in the following way:

"An individual who activates ideas or behaviors that are consistent with each other finds themselves in a satisfying emotional state (cognitive consonance); conversely, they will encounter discriminatory and elaborative difficulties if the two representations are opposed or divergent. This inconsistency is what produces cognitive dissonance, which the individual automatically seeks to eliminate or reduce due to the significant psychological discomfort it entails (e.g., reduced self-esteem); this can lead to the activation of various elaborative processes that allow for the compensation of dissonance (and restoration of self-esteem)"

[https://en.wikipedia.org/wiki/Cognitive_dissonance]

In very simple words... in certain situations, a specific act is horrible, reprehensible, and as such should be judged and repudiated; in others, however, that same act becomes justifiable, acceptable, tolerable, almost... necessary. And I will build reasons for myself so that this *ethi-*

cal justification of the act becomes absolutely effective and protects my self-esteem.

So what is *cognitive dissonance*? How can I define *bipolar ethics*? Is it the castle of justifications we build to defend ourselves when we have strongly judged the act committed by others? Is it the self-absolution we consider necessary, especially when we have been extremely... puritanical or fundamentalist in judging others? Can this process be minimized to prevent it from leaving us... suffering? Is there a way out? What can we do to alleviate its effects?

All these questions, which I began to ask myself after glimpsing the dissonant pattern in my daily life, have generated in me a strong desire to communicate, to talk about this topic with other people and maybe one day listen to their experiences, compare myself with them in a very large round table. But let's get to the book.

A book or a short video?

Bipolar ethics is certainly not a neologism, although it is not often that you find these two terms together in books, philosophical treatises, on the web, or in everyday conversation.

What you have chosen to read and now have in your hands or on your screen is not an essay, it cannot be one given my purely empirical competence in fields such as sociology and psychology; it is not a novel, although I would perhaps like to write one someday; it is not even a... book, at least in the strict sense of the term.

When the idea of writing *Bipolar Ethics* was born, as was appropriate, I first tried to understand if the topic had already been thoroughly explored by others and, if so, how many times it had been addressed. I navigated the web, book e-shops, starting with the search for the terms "ethics," "bipolar," "dissonance," "cognitive," used in various ways.

The search did not yield many results.

With courage, I then tried to imagine this book and, shortly thereafter, I began to note a possible structure for the index, the chapters until I quickly found myself starting to write it.

But when I reread what I had written, I felt a strong sense of... boredom. I wanted to identify a more engaging expressive mode that would reconcile a classic topic for psychological studies - interesting, of course, but which risks being boring indeed - with the pleasure of reading. This was no easy task.

I jotted down notes that I then revised and deleted continually, always remaining extremely disappointed. I asked myself an endless series of questions without easily finding useful answers. I was going through one of those phases where you wait for the right idea, but the idea just doesn't come!

What to do to make it all more interesting, convincing, and at the same time agile, dynamic, fast, easily accessible and quickly usable? Is there a middle ground between a *tome*, a *doorstop* essay and a super quick and immediate *short video*? Is it possible to somehow get the reader passionate about the book? Can both young people, used to short content, and older people, more accustomed to... *tomes*, be involved at the same time?

I love reading, creative writing, music, acting, and performances of all kinds. This mix of passions pushed me in a direction that, initially, I couldn't grasp at all. Yet something was beginning to move...

We have been living for decades in the era of *social networks*, *short contents* and *videos*, *reels*, *bite-sized news*, and text messages fragmented into small parts. A huge 270-page book written by a perfect stranger, in addition to being difficult to conceive, would have had no chance of success. It is now clear how young *digital natives* often have a very *low attention span*; but even our generation, the so-called *digital immigrants*, now has the same problem! A video or a text that asks the user to stay focused for more than 5 minutes is universally considered too boring to be enjoyed.

But then, after much thought, from this desire to experiment with something new, a real *epiphany* suddenly emerged: to write a book that was not only simply *understandable*, but could be read... quickly, even in a *non-continuous way* and, like a short video, independently of the chosen page.

In this book, in fact, every *pair of pages* is self-sufficient, although tied to the book by the obvious common thread. Each *pair of pages* represents a paragraph, and the paragraph begins and ends in that same pair of pages.

And each pair of pages reports a case of real and ordinary life, something easily imaginable and at the same time performable and, why not, even set to music, using each paragraph of this book as material for a fusion between arts and imagining it as if it were written, read, listened to, sung, performed at the same time. This book should not be read in sequence. It could turn out to be terribly boring! Ideally, you should open it at random, read the two facing pages, then close it and reopen it to read another part.

Each paragraph tells, on the left page, the adventures of a protagonist with an imaginary name, who lives, evaluates, judges, acts, in an ordinary and at the same time particular situation, relating to the event with a certain *ethical, moral, judgmental polarity*; the same paragraph then tells, on the next right page, how the same protagonist in a similar situation, but in a different role, completely reverses decisions, judgments, and actions, adhering to a sort of diametrically opposite *polarity*.

The characters have imaginary names and represent the many counterparts who live the same situations in everyday life. There are many of them! My desire, in fact, was to ignite in the reader the self-awareness that this phenomenology concerns us all. Recognizing oneself in even some of these episodes can be a first step towards a deeper knowledge of oneself. It was for me.

Learning to recognize the moment when you are about to go from *sacrificial victim* to *ruthless judge* becomes fundamental in a process of transformation and rebirth that can really lead to two very important results: the first, individual, as there would be a moderation of the dissonant phenomenology, with consequent alleviation of induced suffering and a progressive improvement in the quality of life; the second, global, because a less... dissonant humanity is also more understanding, inclusive, tolerant, generous.

I hope I have hit the target: to ignite even in a single reader a glimmer at the end of the tunnel that illuminates the deep divide between what we really are and what we believe we are, between what we affirm and defend and the way we act every day.

Before starting this journey

The chapters will unfold following a list of cases, in some of which, I hope, the reader will recognize themselves. With the chapter '**In the Car**', we will start *gently*, analyzing some examples of cognitive dissonance that can occur on the road, while driving a vehicle or walking. We will then move on to '**Religion and Devotion**', examining the often dissonant behaviors of religious individuals. In the chapter '**Ecology**', we will focus on one of today's most important fields, and one in which the dissonances are numerous and interesting. The chapter '**World of work**', long and detailed, reports examples from the corporate life of various professionals, with their baggage of inconsistency. In '**State, politics, services**', we will personify the concept of the State, of Government, highlighting its extreme dissonances. And so on, throughout the book, passing through the chapters '**Society**', '**Love and Sexuality**', '**Peoples and Cultures**', and concluding on a high note with '**Your Neighbor**'.

I am quite sure that the reader will recognize themselves, if not in all, in many of the examples discussed. Indeed, we are all affected by *cognitive dissonance*, but it is difficult to understand and recognize the phenomenon. Yet the evidence is there, in our days, in our hours, in our activities, in our choices, at work, at school, on the road, in politics.

To start, in the next paragraph we will analyze two particular cases in more detail than the rest of the book.

In these two cases, we will define the 'exogenous situation' as one where we assume an ethical, pure, and rigorous polarity, believing that a wrong has been committed by others. On the other hand, we will define the 'endogenous situation' as one where we are the 'guilty' ones, but we absolve ourselves without any apparent hesitation.

As we progress through the pages, this specification will no longer be necessary. The reader will automatically identify the two situations. And if this, sooner or later, starts to happen in your lives as well, if you begin to recognize the described polarities, this book will have made sense.

Happy reading!

Roberto

Methodological Approach

Before delving into the briefly described cases, let's select 2 examples, from the long list related to *drivers*, in order to allow us to examine in detail the method used in the book.

The subsequent examples will be addressed in a more concise manner but with the same approach.

1 Parking

Situation A (exogenous)

You are on the road, driving your car in the right lane. The road is narrow, and there are cars parked poorly on your side. Maneuvering is difficult, requiring constant slaloming and pauses to allow oncoming traffic from the opposite lane to pass.

At one point, a car ahead of you in the same direction as yours poorly pulls over, occupying almost the entire lane. You immediately realize that your car won't fit in the remaining space... At least not without risks. And you're not willing to take those risks because you know yourself well... you know that when you're forced to make quick, difficult maneuvers, you often end up bumping, denting, or scraping the car. This time, you're determined not to let that happen.

Confidently, you wait for the right door of the stopped car ahead of you to open, expecting someone to get out, hoping it's not a slow, elderly person. But no one exits the car; everything remains silent and still as it was at the beginning of time. And most importantly, no one seems to care about you or your time. You start to get quite irritated...

Let's define a parameter that we'll use from now on to gauge the amount of angry impulse that pervades our being. We'll call this parameter "anger saturation." Let's define it with a touch of irony:

Anger Saturation

noun.. – **1.** Percentage of anger clouding the human mind. Inversely proportional to the ability to think clearly. Initially set at 10%, but can quickly exceed 70% after particularly irritating events. In rare cases, the value can exceed the 98th percentile. During such moments, serious episodes of violence can occur. From now on, we will denote this as "AS".

The car in front of yours has stopped to wait for someone who evidently isn't nearby! Through the windows of both cars, you focus and see the silhouette of the driver moving slowly against the light. They don't seem particularly concerned about causing inconvenience. They pick up their smartphone, then put it down, rearrange the groceries in the bag beside them... Your AS (anger saturation) is at 20%.

You honk the horn to notify the driver that it's impossible to pass. For a moment, they glance at the rearview mirror, then look towards the sidewalk and ignore the warning. Your AS suddenly jumps to 40% and then to 70%.

Then something incredible happens... the drivers behind you start honking too, and you feel a strong sense of solidarity. Enthusiastic and happy to discover that your cause has a group of supporters, you feel empowered to assert your justified right to pass!

Now that others are on your side, you press even harder on the horn to urge the driver blocking the road to move their car. At some point, you hear from outside, "Man... are you moving? Go ahead! What are you waiting for?".

Suddenly, doubt creeps in, and you decide to poke your head out to understand more... and you discover that the driver behind is clearly gesturing that there's enough space for a massive 86-wheel truck to pass through the remaining lane, meaning it's actually YOU blocking the passage.

Suddenly, you realize that the line of drivers, now resembling the queue at the toll booth in Rimini the day before August 15th, are honking, but at you!

And so, from hunter to hunted. Embarrassed, you try to reassess the situation and timidly start moving the car again, but you quickly realize that the space is really tight! At this point, your thoughts bounce between two extremes: either get out and challenge the driver behind to drive my car past the obstacle, or honk the horn endlessly to shift the focus back to the one who obstructed me.

You choose the latter option, with an AS of 80%, using all your strength to press the horn with both arms. You hear the trumpets of judgment... This time, they'll move...!

The driver shows that their AS has gone from 20% to 40%. But they don't move. They get out of the car. You can already imagine the worst... a fight is about to break out. But no, they calmly position themselves in front of the passage and signal that a cruise ship, one of the big ones, can pass through there.

You're at your wit's end, with an AS of 85%, when suddenly you catch a friendly gesture from the frantic driver. They wave their hands to facilitate your passage.

Despite wondering why the best choice for them wasn't simply to park better, you accept the help, and your AS drops to 75%. A couple of maneuvers later, you're through. And you wonder why you didn't realize on your own that passing was possible and within your reach.

Why did your mind initially suggest that you couldn't get through? Why did others perceive that passage was possible even though it wasn't easy? You're there thinking and rethinking what happened when suddenly you realize that passage was always possible, but you couldn't tolerate how easily someone deliberately decided to restrict your progress. Instead of adapting, being pragmatic, and available, you decided that such an affront couldn't be tolerated. All of this altered your perception of severity to the point where the space seemed truly narrow, the affront truly intolerable, the blockage absolute.

Situation B (endogenous)

A few days later, you find yourself on the same street, roles reversed. You need to wait and pick up someone dear to you, perhaps your mother or father who may have difficulty walking, or your child in a stroller. In short, you **really** need to park at that spot. Behind you, a line of cars driven by impatient motorists. To your right, poorly parked cars occupy part of your lane. You think to yourself... if they can do it, so can I. What harm could I possibly cause? My car won't block the road more than theirs, and it will only be there for a few minutes. So, confident in the absolute, total, valid, indisputable, urgent emergency you find yourself in, you don't hesitate for a moment to park double-parked in the first available space.

A car passes you, which reassures you because in the end, passage is easy, so what do you care, others will pass too. But at some point, a driver starts honking repeatedly, but you're reasonably sure they're not honking at you, but someone else.

You pretend not to notice and look elsewhere, trying to keep your composure, but the horn resounds loud and commanding. Finally, you turn around and realize the driver is honking at you to move. Your AS is at 65%. Inside you, the emergency you find yourself in echoes, the absolute need to have your car there, and you would like to get out and explain to the driver that you cannot park far away risking leaving a child alone waiting. You are in the right, without a doubt; anyone who knew what you were doing and why, would not hesitate for a moment to agree with you. But you can't explain it to the drivers in line. So, you decide to get out of the car to at least talk to the first driver, who is performing a concert with a bass horn in B-flat minor. As you get out, however, you realize that there is space for the cars in line to pass... it's there!

You start giving directions to the driver to help them pass through the ample space you've left. In the end, they pass, but others follow, and not everyone may be willing to try. And behind them is a truck that won't be able to pass unless you park elsewhere.

Fortunately, the person you are waiting for arrives, gets into your car, and you can drive off and avoid a brawl. You find yourself with an AS of 55%, cursing the impatience of the motorists.

Cognitive dissonance

This example is already indicative of the thesis itself of this book, implicitly reiterated in each of its chapters and paragraphs. Depending on the situation you find yourself in, the criterion for evaluating your actions and those of others can change for you in a... polar or even multipolar manner.

A clarification is necessary, although it is implicitly deducible. Considering these episodes exclusively as bipolar is merely a simplification required for the flow of the text and for a straightforward narration of the examples. It is clear that there can be more than two polarities, all mutually antithetical or even partially consonant and partially dissonant. We proceed with the simplification based on two polarities among them dissonant, leaving the reader the freedom to identify and recognize multipolar examples.

In situations where you are the one who absolutely needs to pass, regardless of the actual urgency, your actions are imbued with an ethical aura in your favor, leading you to stigmatize the lack of respect from reckless parkers who cause delays in the flow of traffic, disrupting the schedules of everyone affected.

And who knows, perhaps in a *sliding doors* phenomenology, that delay could cause irreparable damage. It is deeply unjust that someone who parks in such a manner, obstructing everyone, can remain indifferent to the harm caused. It's absurd that such things happen.

However, if you find yourself as the driver who needs to park, you perceive your actions, though diametrically opposed, as still ethically correct. Those who disrespect you now are the drivers in the queue, who should understand that the only reason compelling you to park in that manner is an evident emergency, such as picking up an elderly person who cannot walk to your car if it were parked far away, or a child who cannot safely cross the street alone.

It's deeply unjust for them to honk and push you to move your car.

It's ethically wrong for them to remain indifferent to your problem.

In the same situation, reversed, you still feel justified. You feel you have absolute reasons and are being treated unfairly. You invoke a polarity in your behavior that unfortunately changes depending on the situation.

If someone parks blocking traffic or makes it impossible for you to park in your designated spot, or occupies multiple parking spots, you become furious.

If you see someone parked in a disabled parking area, you are shocked by their insensitivity. If you see a car parked on the side of the road, you are amazed by the folly that led that driver to park there.

But if you have to carry out a task that you consider crucial at that moment, like buying two €1 lottery tickets or purchasing rear sun-shades for your car, then anyone who obstructs you or rightfully claims their parking space will be seen as *impatient and overbearing*.

This is cognitive dissonance, this is bipolar ethics.

Now let's look at another example, still related to cars and roads.

2 Overtaking

Situation A (exogenous)

You are driving along a two-way road without a divider, fairly busy in your direction of travel. There are a few cars coming from the opposite direction, which pose a risk for any overtaking maneuver.

The center line is dashed at various points, making overtaking possible if timed and executed carefully. You are in the car with your spouse and your three children.

You overtake a few cars cautiously and continue steadily towards your destination.

At one point, a truck enters your lane behind you from an entrance. The truck's speed strictly adheres to the highway code, and the truck driver seems to be following all the rules.

You glance in the rearview mirror behind the truck and intermittently see the headlights of a car... impatiently peering out whenever oncoming traffic permits.

You realize that the driver of the car directly behind the truck is impatient to overtake, but obviously when they attempt to peek out for overtaking, they realize it would cause a head-on collision and retract.

This process repeats so many times that you can sense the rising AS (anger saturation) from that driver at a distance.

Your own judgment is already harsh: it's too dangerous, frontal collisions are deadly, if they start overtaking and can't pull back, we could all be involved in the crash. They're reckless, a madman, and so on.

As the driver's car reaches an AS of 95%, they suddenly make a daring overtaking move at the most dangerous point, uphill and approaching a blind curve with zero visibility. You cross your fingers hoping not to be caught in the very likely accident.

The car completes the overtaking maneuver without major issues; no cars from the opposite direction appear.

They were very lucky! You and everyone who witnessed the scene unleash a barrage of curses at the reckless driver. You notice there are children in their car too! Reckless lunatic!

Your anger is incredible; your AS is at 80%... you curse them, even though they can't hear you, predicting they won't live long if they keep this up, wishing them the worst of the worst (but not death, you don't go that far, their recklessness will take care of that).

Inexplicably, you accelerate, almost wanting to catch up to them, even though deep down, you feel foolish driving at such a slow speed.

You realize your car is pathetic compared to the monster on wheels that took the risk. In your mind, you even start judging others as snobs and elitists.

You create an image of the other driver that verges on that of a *galactic mega-dictator* from the Fantozzi series, and you even go beyond, imagining them as autocratic and... bloodthirsty!

Situation B (endogenous)

You are in your car with your family, on the same road as in the previous story, facing the same traffic conditions and dangers of overtaking, along with the frequent curves that often limit visibility.

Suddenly, from a side road a few hundred meters ahead of your car, an extremely slow truck enters the road in the same direction as you. You are in a hurry, and not just any hurry... Your hurry is justified!

You need to reach friends who have invited you for dinner by the time they specified. You've never liked being late; you detest arriving when everyone is already at the table, unable to lend a hand with preparations or exchange a few words while cooking. No, arriving when dinner begins is terribly rude, and you cannot allow it.

Indeed, these are absolute, incontrovertible reasons, and that damned slow, gigantic truck threatens to ruin everything. Before it appeared, you were neither too fast nor too slow, but you would have surely arrived at least 15 minutes before dinner, which wouldn't have been much, but at least you wouldn't have appeared incompetent, tarnishing your reputation as a respectable punctual person.

But now, that mountain of iron is there... insurmountable, impassable... or nearly so.

Weighing all your reasons, convinced that they take absolute precedence over safety, traffic laws, your life, your family's lives, and those of other drivers, you decide that you really cannot afford to stay behind, helplessly watching the minutes pass.

And so, you move away a bit from the truck to gain visibility, glance far ahead, and despite seeing a blind curve, you decide there's enough space. You shift down to second gear, the engine roars triumphantly, you signal, swerve, and in an instant, you're in the other lane with the massive truck passing on your right.

The curve approaches, and with it, death in the form of likely oncoming cars. But you press down on the pedal!

It's a kind of Russian roulette. But come on! Statistics clearly say it's not certain there will be a car coming right at that moment. It'll be fine.

Your family is terrified, as are the other drivers; you see their shocked faces through their windshields, looking at you fearfully... if they could get out of their cars, they'd beat you to a pulp... but outwardly, you show calmness, even though you're dying inside.

Finally, you manage to overtake the truck, get back in time, pass the curve, see that the next car is still far away, and even manage to pretend you're calm, saying there was plenty of time!

101 examples

Here is what you will find in this book... 101 brief examples of symmetric situations from daily life where, in a very short time span, we are first victims and then executioners, first judges and then defendants.

Meanwhile, the inner and painful screech of cognitive dissonance makes us suffer deeply.

Gamification: assess ethical bipolarity

The paragraphs in this book total 101. Let's set aside the last *bonus* paragraph for a moment and focus on the remaining 100 to empirically gauge our percentage of... ethical bipolarity.

However, it's not necessary to have experienced all the described situations. We might have only lived through one *polarity* of the experience, or it could be so far from our usual habits that it's completely inapplicable. In any case, we can engage in an exercise of empathy: imagining ourselves in the shoes of the story's protagonist, trying to understand how we would react if we were in that situation, what sensations we would feel, which feelings would prevail, and what actions would arise.

Putting ourselves in the protagonist's shoes with the same honesty with which we should read this entire book requires great authenticity on our part, leading us to admit what we truly feel deep down in our hearts.

Remember, the aim of this book is to recognize within ourselves the recurring process that leads most or all of us to act in ethically dissonant, ethically bipolar ways.

Through empathy, even imagining ourselves as the leader of a sovereign state undergoing bombardment by a neighboring country isn't that difficult. It might take a few extra minutes to immerse ourselves in the character's feelings, desires, impulses, and defensive instincts.

At the end of each chapter, you'll find a table like the one below as an example. In the first column, we'll list the titles of the paragraphs from the concluded chapter; in the second column, with a checkmark next to the considered paragraph, you can assign yourself 0 points each time you recognize yourself in only one of the two experiences,

A **or** B. With a checkmark in the third column, however, you'll assign yourself 1 point each time you recognize yourself in both situations, A **and** B.

Paragraph	Only A OR B	Both A AND B
1 Paragraph title	■ 0 points	☐ 1 point
2 Paragraph title	☐ 0 points	■ 1 point
TOTAL		1 point

Please place only one checkmark per paragraph. To summarize:

- **1 point** at each paragraph where we have experienced (or empathized with and recognized ourselves in) both polarities of judgment and action;

- **0 points** at each paragraph where we have experienced (or empathized with and recognized ourselves in) only one of the two polarities of judgment and action;

Next to the title of each paragraph, you will find a letter, A on the left side and B on the right side. You can place a checkmark or a tick on one or both of them, either to remind yourself that you've already read that pair of pages or to note that you have experienced, identified with, or related to one or both experiences. One or no ticks for the same experience will count as 0 points. Two ticks for the same experience will count as 1 point.

In the end, by adding up all the points from the 100 experiences, you will get a number between 0 and 100, which will roughly represent the frequency of our experience of ethical bipolarity relative to the various paragraphs, in percentage terms.

And this will help us understand even more about ourselves!

Gamification 1/10

Paragraph	Only A OR B	Both A AND B
1 Parking	☐ 0 points	☐ 1 point
2 Overtaking	☐ 0 points	☐ 1 point
TOTAL		

In the car

The other day, two guys in a car rear-ended me, and I said to them, "Go forth and multiply", but not in those exact words.

Woody Allen

3 Right of way [A]

Piersimona, 6:00 PM on any given day

I can feel your frustration with drivers who don't respect the "give way" sign. Let's put it plainly: it's a triangular sign, and if it's true that everyone who drives a car has passed a driving test, then everyone should know it! But let's get to the real meaning of the sign: it "requires giving way to vehicles on the intersecting road, both from the right and from the left." I want to shout this at every crazy driver who cuts me off anywhere... "requires"... it's an actual requirement! It doesn't mean "go ahead if you feel like it", or "go ahead because you have the right", it means you are obligated to stop to let me pass when I approach that intersection! You must stop absolutely if you en-counter that sign. What part of this sentence isn't clear? You have to stop, do you understand? 99% of the time you have to brake, stop your vehicle, slam on the brakes… how else do I need to explain it? It's not a stop sign, sure. But you can only proceed without stopping if there is no one approaching from the road you are crossing. So, if I'm on the main road and you're merging, what's under your wheels isn't a runway... it's the space where you can and must stop to let those approach-ing pass safely! But seriously! Every time I encounter one of these, and it happens several times a day, I honk, flash my lights, I try in every way to make them understand that what they're doing is illegal, dangerous, reckless. And maybe I have the overtaking lane occupied by other cars and I can't even move over. I have to brake hard, hoping the one behind me doesn't rear-end me. In short, not respecting the "give way" sign is truly extremely dangerous!

Right of way [B]

Piersimona, 7:50 AM on another ordinary day

I didn't hear my alarm and I'm in a monstrous rush. I risk being late for the office, which I can't afford today because we have some important clients visiting. We often receive such visits, it's true, but today is different: we need to present our new product to them. I'm in the car now, merging onto the highway from the acceleration lane. I check the left mirror. I see a car approaching in the lane I'm about to merge into, and another vehicle overtaking it. They have plenty of space, there's no need to slow down, I'll merge smoothly. At worst, the vehicle in the right lane, passed by the one on the left, can move to the passing lane and overtake me without issues. I hit the gas and in an instant, I'm on the highway. But wait, what? The vehicle behind me is approaching fast! He's flashing his lights, honking the horn! Why? Suddenly, I take my foot off the accelerator to understand better, but he swerves and that's when I realize the danger he's putting everyone in. The other car finishes its pass on the left and he abruptly moves into the passing lane. He catches up to me, overtakes me while hurling curses after curses. What the hell is this idiot complaining about? I signaled, slowed down briefly on the lane, and then, making sure everything was clear, I went. He had space to move, brake, accelerate... what does he want? He can't drive and it's certainly not my fault. Besides, I had the 'give way' sign, not a stop sign. Stop signs make me stop; 'give way' signs allow me to go. Enough, I don't want this incompetent ruining my day. I need to get to the office quickly, and my morning is much, much more important than his.

4 The traffic light [A]

Alfio, 8:30 AM on any given day

I find it absurd the way drivers of all kinds and ages approach intersections controlled by traffic lights. It's like being on the starting grid of a Formula 1 Grand Prix. There's the guy on the powerful motorcycle who revs up and takes off like a rocket, those who compete to move first as if they were sitting on a Ferrari instead of miserable micro cars with pathetic engines. There's the one in the supercar who starts off slowly and then halfway through the intersection floors the accelerator to make the roar heard by the plebeians around. And then there are those who, in defiance of every rule of the road, go through on yellow about to turn red, even on red, endangering everyone on the intersecting road. Is it really so dangerous to behave like this, do they realize? Life is short and a careless moment like this is all it takes to risk it all! It just happened to me... I was stopped in my modest car at the traffic light waiting for green. After what felt like an eternity, the light eventually changed. I calmly started, shifting gears and accelerating gently! But halfway through the intersection, what happens? A road pirate comes from the right at full speed! I manage to avoid him by a hair's breadth. He's one of those reckless drivers who, while the traffic light is still 300 meters away, instead of slowing down, accelerates to get through before it turns red. He succeeds, but because the intersection is huge, he reaches the middle while cars from the other street have already started moving. And this lunatic is convinced that his haste justifies the risk of serious accidents! It's madness. And never does a traffic officer come to fine these reckless drivers. And then we hear daily reports of war regarding deaths from road accidents. Unbelievable!

The traffic light [B]

Alfio, 3:30 PM on another ordinary day

I'm in a crazy rush, like never before today! I left the office early to see my accountant Felippo who needs additional information for my tax return. I forgot to include all the receipts and invoices, and today is the last day to submit the documentation. I'm in a hurry! I see from afar the intersection on Via degli Eremiti. It's a terrible traffic light, red lasts forever! Hopefully, the green light stays on a bit longer. As expected... yellow! And I'm far from the intersection. Damn it, today I'm seriously late and I can't delay my commitment. I try to accelerate, hoping that the yellow will last just long enough for me to cross to the other side. After all, if the red lasts so long, perhaps the yellow will too. There are still 100 meters to go and the yellow is still there. The other side of the intersection seems so far away. And then the traffic light, just a few meters from me, inevitably turns red. It's too late to stop, but I'm sure the drivers on the right and left won't be quick enough to enter the intersection while I'm crossing. But then... one of those crazies who think the traffic light is the starting grid for a car race zooms past and in an instant reaches the middle. A lunatic... almost hits me head-on. I steer to avoid him and end up on the sidewalk refuge in the middle of the intersection. And that madman, not content, curses at me, I can see it in the mirror. What? I went through on yellow and it's allowed when you can't stop. And you? You who start with your Fruto 1.2 as if you're driving a Frattalpini 3500 twin-turbo? Do you have any idea of the danger you put both of us in? I have an unavoidable appointment, one that I can't miss. But you? No! You're just insane, nothing more.

5 Speed limits [A]

Daphne, 6:15 PM on any given day

A madman just raced down this street from the intersection I'm about to cross on foot. And now I'm practically paralyzed with fear! Not a madman in the strict and common sense of the term, but a lunatic behind the wheel of a car. An idiot who, sensing from afar that the traffic light was about to turn green, accelerated and, to top it off, upon reaching the intersection, turned left without slowing down in the slightest. His pathetic little car, which if you buy it new from the dealership they pay you to take it, barely held the curve and only thanks to a miraculous balance between centrifugal force and centripetal force did it not flip over, veer off the road, and strike us terrified pedestrians. A perfect idiot, one of those whose micro-brain, compared to which a chicken is Einstein, doesn't even remotely grasp the possibility of ending up in the middle of a manslaughter trial! One of those who thinks he's Fruiss Badminton driving his Monstrari F 3042. But do I really have to resign myself to the fact that leaving the house means risking not coming back because of an imbecile like this? And then, can someone explain why he behaves like this? Despite not liking gender stereotypes, most of these idiots are dim-witted males! Don't you understand that there's nothing manly about flexing your little idiotic right foot to lower the accelerator? There's nothing heroic about it; even kids can do it! Or perhaps you had an urgent commitment? So urgent that it makes manslaughter acceptable? I don't believe there's anything in the world that should take precedence over a person's life, that could make these extremely risky actions forgivable. You are reckless!

Speed limits [B]

Daphne, 6:42 AM on another ordinary day

I'm in serious trouble today. I forgot my shift at the hospital. It's my turn this Saturday, and as much as I don't feel like it, I have to be on the ward by 7:00 AM. What do I do now? I didn't hear the first alarm or the second. I heard the third one, but it rings much later! I found myself staring blankly at the clock before realizing the drama, wondering for several seconds what day it was. My first, hopeful thought was for a... day off. Then slowly, the terrible truth dawned on me. And I began a mad dash to get ready as quickly as possible. Now, panting, I rush down the stairs and get into my car. Guess what? Damn it! Almost out of gas! So, I sprint to the gas station, cutting in front of the customer ahead of me and risking lynching, make a quick prayer gesture, and get away with it. Finally, I'm on the highway heading to the hospital. I press the pedal... 100, 110. I know. The speed limit on this road is 90 km/h, but how can I obey it? I really can't today; it's too important. I care about getting promoted, and I can't mess this up! What would happen if I arrived late and that arrogant Porfiria ran to the chief physician like the squalid informer she is? No, today I'm justified in speeding. But I don't want to cause an accident and hurt someone. After all, I don't have a Straforghini Murtellago, just a simple and microscopic Brancia Mupsillon, with tiny wheels like this. But I'm sure my trusty car won't let me down. I race, overtake, change lanes everywhere. Please forgive me, but I have a serious motivation. Now I'm taking that curve at 110, brrr. I grip the steering wheel with my fingertips, as if sneezing would make the car lose contact with the asphalt. Curve passed, I continue. I can't avoid this race. My job is on the line!

6 Driving and smartphones [A]

Alfonso, 11:30 AM on any given day

I'm out running family errands in my car, and suddenly I see behind me, in the driving lane on SS354, a dark compact car speeding up and showing no signs of overtaking to pass me. I glance in the rearview mirror and notice the driver is focused on their smartphone. They hold it up high, almost towards the mirror, and still haven't noticed me! I dare to honk the horn in hopes that they'll realize, eventually, that it's meant for them, but nothing. I'm afraid to switch lanes myself because if they decide to do it too, there might still be a collision. The person briefly lifts their eyes from the smartphone, finally notices me, and calmly swerves, overtakes, and moves ahead, narrowly avoiding me! They're reckless! People like them should have their licenses revoked! It's become a routine now, every time you're stopped at a traffic light and it turns green, the car in front of you doesn't move. And why not? You can immediately tell by their silhouette against the backlight through the car's rear window. They're looking at their smartphone, holding it in their right hand. Probably texting personal messages on VazzApp or posting on Pacegram! Damn it, this is extremely dangerous! Do they realize the risk? Besides being absolutely prohibited by the traffic code. Maybe it's a bit less so when you're stopped at a light, but the habit leads to doing it anytime and anywhere, even on highways or motorways. And they all think they can manage it without any problems! They believe just glancing up every four seconds is enough to steer the car and continue smoothly. But so much can happen in those four seconds. You can kill someone and ruin your life forever...

Driving and smartphones [B]

Alfonso, 4:30 PM on another ordinary day

I'm rushing from one office to another within the company for fairly urgent activities. The new project is experiencing a moment of strong growth and I'm at the center of this process with my cross-functional skills. In the past, professionals were required to have specific vertical knowledge, but now the more you know, the better. The boss is demanding, but not very technically competent. I often have to explain and re-explain what I'm doing, how I'm managing my time, and many other things. He often presses with questions and being naturally restless, I feel a strong urgency to respond. Right now, I'm in the company car and I really need to get to the other office where I can complete the final test that I need to finish this week's tasks. Then, in 3 hours, I have a plane that will take me to the partner company's headquarters. I'm speeding along Lilliputian Street, my vehicle doesn't exceed 45 km/h. It's a straight road, so I glance at my smartphone and the chat for a moment, just a moment though, I definitely don't want to speed or endanger anyone. I manage to read a message from my boss questioning the validity of the test I'm about to perform. What? I was absolutely clear in explaining its results! The pedal is to the metal, but the intersection is still far away. The traffic light is green so there are no issues. I decide to send a short message. But no, it's not safe to do it while driving. I search for the microphone icon, glance at the traffic light, and plan my maneuver to continue driving. I start recording the message. Yes, I know, it's not allowed, it's dangerous, but this is really important, it's a work urgency! I begin recording the message, I cross the intersection and for a moment glance at the phone while speaking to respond and clarify that I'm not... CRASH

7 The accelerator [A]

Amedeo, 7:45 AM on any given day

What absurdity these races at the traffic light on Via Dei Virgulti. It's incomprehensible for what mental folly some individuals mistake the asphalt behind the red light for an F1 starting grid. You see them there, challenging each other head to head, yet without looking at one another. The car fronts inch forward as the clutch starts to engage, then slide back a bit, knowing the traffic light will still take a while. Then the light turns green, clutches release, tires squeal, it sounds like a race track at Bronza rather than a suburban street in a mediocre city in an equally mediocre corner of the universe. The two cars in front of me take off, neck and neck, almost level. From behind, I see the heads of the two drivers, filled only with their own foolishness and the desire to vent their anger and need for revenge on the asphalt and their 'rival', pervading their utterly mediocre lives. And on top of it all, I see them taking senseless risks with the same nonchalance. Yes, because after the traffic light, there's an intersection with a mandatory left turn onto Via Lesmi. The two cars reach the point where they both must turn. Their respective drivers try to stay side by side without yielding. And I say yielding because inevitably one of them must yield, since the lane they are entering is much narrower than the one they're coming from. Consequently, only one will go first, relieved of the resentment they carry towards life; the other will go after, with their rage cranked up to the max. Absurd... I really don't understand these things at all! Putting the lives of other drivers, pedestrians, cyclists at risk... for what? To be first at the next traffic light...? To win what prize?

The accelerator [B]

Amedeo, 1:05 PM on another ordinary day

I'm at the traffic light on Via Dei Virgulti, the one that leads me to Via Lesmi. I need to rush to lunch at my parents' place and I have very little time... the company doesn't allow more than an hour for lunch break. It would be nice, in an ideal world, if employees could manage their break as they see fit, and make up for it later, but it's not like that. I stop in the right lane and look at the clock: it's 1:06 PM. Ugh. No matter how hard I try to leave the office at exactly 1:00, I never manage to get to my parents' before 1:20. And then? Twenty minutes to eat in a hurry and another twenty to get back. What a crazy hassle... but I really want to visit them every day. A car pulls up to my left and passes me by a bit. I glance over and see... practically a stereotype! Here's some sort of tycoon in diapers with an expensive car, suit, and oversized watch. He looks at me with condescension while talking on the phone, convinced he's deciding the fate of the world. He accelerates and brakes, starting that typical clutch-brake-and-accelerator back-and-forth of someone who wants to show the world what they're made of. What a big idiot. As if a fancy car and all its accessories prove a person's worth. But never mind all these discussions. I press the brake and remain perfectly still. I let him vent, ignore him, I'm not interested in these childish games. Let him keep his pathetic 20-centimeter lead... I'm not interested in racing him. But then, I look at the traffic light and, I don't know why, as soon as it turns green I release the clutch and hit the accelerator, starting the most formulaic turn of my life. The shift from first to second lasts just a few milliseconds. The result? I'm ahead and he can do nothing to catch up. I look at him in the mirror and enjoy it, oh boy do I enjoy it. Brrrrr.

8 Emergency lanes ^A

Adelaide, 5:00 PM on any given day

And here I am again, stuck in this damned state road that every blessed day is plagued by construction, accidents, potholes, etc. Every time I see a stoplight even at a distance, I slow down to avoid rear-ending the last car in line. And today, here I am stopped in traffic again. Hundreds of cars ahead of me, maybe thousands behind me. This time it's because of an accident, which always fills me with dread. It might be minor, but generally thinking of someone trapped in a car waiting for an ambulance terrifies me. I wish the emergency response could arrive immediately from above, with a helicopter landing next to the vehicles involved. We're moving at a snail's pace. At one point, despite being absolutely prohibited by traffic regulations, some idiot behind me rockets to the right and takes over the emergency lane. Are you serious? Do you know that's the only access route for the emergency services who are definitely on their way to help today's unfortunate person? I mean, are you out of your mind? He approaches and has the audacity to honk the horn so that I move a bit to the left to let him pass more easily. I mean, do you realize what you're doing? Do you know that if the ambulance arrives now and can't get through, you would be at fault if someone involved in the accident dies? And you don't care about the other drivers who, like me, respect traffic laws by patiently waiting in line until the emergency services arrive? Do you have any idea how risky your maneuver is for the people involved in the crash, or for others who might be involved in other accidents? I mean, you absolute jerk, do you understand at least a bit how stupid your actions are? I hope you can come to your senses and realize this before causing another disaster!

Emergency lanes [B]

Adelaide, 7:45 AM on another ordinary day

Once again, crawling at a snail's pace on this damned highway. It's surely due to ongoing roadworks or an accident, as always. However, I absolutely must be at my lawyer's office by 7:50 AM so I can be in my office by 8:00 AM to finish by 5:00 PM and make it to the 5:30 PM premiere of the 3rd remake of 'The Devil wears Prague'. I've taken all the side roads and shortcuts possible, but I'm stuck in this long, slow queue for the last stretch. Damn it! If only these other idiot drivers could organize themselves better and drive more decently, if they started earlier and braked later, there wouldn't be any problems. But they're incapable, people who got their driver's license as a charity from an examiner who just wanted to get rid of them to go have fun. And the worst part is, surely none of them have a valid reason for reaching their destination. They're mostly just loafing around, not like professionals who, like me, after a hard day's work, want to unwind a bit. The exit from the ring road is close, the deceleration lane will open soon. I've made up my mind, I'll take the emergency lane and do everyone a favor! I'm certainly not overtaking the other cars improperly; they're surely here to go straight, while I need to exit. Even if an emergency vehicle were to come through this lane now, I wouldn't obstruct it because in a few hundred meters, I can move to the right and get out of the way. I'm in a real hurry! I cover the first 200 meters smoothly. But now there's an idiot with their car significantly shifted to the right. I honk the horn. They gesture as if to say, 'Where are you going?' Idiot, I'm exiting, move over!

9 Thunderstorms [A]

Alice, 2:25 PM on any given day

Damn it, the lunch break is almost over. I need to hurry back to the office, only 5 minutes left! It's pouring rain heavily. I'm driving down a boulevard where students from the nearby middle school are dispersing. The boulevard is full of puddles, and it's too late when I realize I can't brake in time, so I hit what feels like a lake and splash two girls walking along the roadside. They start hurling curses and insults at me with remarkable effectiveness. But I didn't mean to get you dirty! Why are you so angry? I apologize with a gesture, I didn't see the puddle in time, I didn't see you in time, if I had braked, the tires would have skidded and maybe I would have hit both of you. Why are you complaining? Why do you keep insulting me, you little incompetents? I'm heading to the office and I'm almost late. Work is serious business, you know? Not like pretending to study for a few hours and then going out with friends. I go back to the office and you go home to eat with mom and then, not caring at all about everything she's prepared for you, without lifting a finger to clean up, in your room chatting for hours. Stop cursing me! I was genuinely sorry before, but now I wish I had literally splashed you, or maybe I'll just circle the block, and if you're still there nursing your wounds, drying off somehow, I'll aim better and transfer the entire contents of the puddle onto your rude faces and your worn-out, raggedy jeans. You don't know what manners are, not at all. Who taught you to express yourselves like this? Figure it out yourselves, you don't deserve any more of my time. I can still make it back to the office in time...

Thunderstorms [B]

Alice, 1:05 PM on another ordinary day

I've just left the office. I'm walking quickly towards the parking lot where my car is. A while ago, a really generous storm broke out! Lots of thunder, lightning, and above all, a lot of rain. Even now, more than an hour later, it's still pouring heavily. As I walk along the company sidewalk, I reach the pedestrian crossing. In the distance, I see a car beginning the curve that will bring it to where I am now. Without hesitation, I walk through a huge puddle because I can't find a dry path that would allow me to cross this real river unscathed. I signal for the car to slow down, pointing to the massive puddle, then to the pedestrian crossing sign, indicating the stripes, but nothing. The idiot doesn't slow down, in fact, he accelerates. At that point, he sees me and, to avoid me, swerves, hitting directly, like something out of ancient annals, the enormous puddle, from which rises a kind of merciless tsunami that engulfs me. In an instant, water is everywhere on my clothes, in my shoes, on my smartphone, in the packet of documents I have with me. Absurd. Look at this idiot, rude and senseless! Does he realize? He literally showered me with filthy water, and now I'm dirty and furious. I curse at him, but in the meantime, he's already driven away. I see his silhouette glancing in the rearview mirror and then he gestures dismissively. What? You're dismissing me? You couldn't care less about manners, show zero regard for others, speed past me in the storm despite my waving, and now I'm the one getting insults? You're truly someone who should be locked up and the key thrown away. You're clueless about where manners belong, one of those people where the fewer there are in the world, the better. Go do whatever useless thing you need to do, worthless man, karma will catch up with you.

10 Crosswalks ^A

Aurelio, 10:00 AM on any given day

I'm on break from work because I urgently need to send a package by this morning. The post office is nearby, so I quickly retrieve the package from my car's trunk in the adjacent parking lot and hurry to reach it. I have to cross Pagnacaudi Avenue, a very, very large street. Midway down the block, right in front of the post office, there are pedestrian crossings. Unfortunately, there are no speed bumps (which I believe should be installed at every pedestrian crossing on the planet Earth), but the crossings are clearly marked. Nevertheless, I don't impose myself on the drivers, I know how it works. I wait for a moment of relative calm and begin to cross. Today, there's a lot of traffic here. As I reach the middle of the roadway, the first driver stops to let me pass. I proceed and... darn it! Some idiot, disregarding the fact that the other driver had clearly stopped to let a pedestrian cross, overtakes from the right and nearly mows me down! I have to step back to avoid ending up as a grotesque heap of guts on the asphalt. What the hell are you doing, you moron! Do you realize you put both of us in danger? You almost tore me to shreds, and you would have been in serious trouble because that would have been vehicular manslaughter! And not just any vehicular manslaughter, one of the worst! Yes, because I'm crossing at the crosswalk and the gentleman to my right stopped, yes... stopped, to let me pass! And what do you do? Crazy and deranged, you shouldn't be driving a car, you should calmly go spend a vacation hugging the core of a very old nuclear power plant. You've taken ten years off my life, you reckless fool!

Crosswalks [B]

Aurelio, 5:15 PM on another random day

I'm in a monstrous hurry, as always. I'm driving down Via dei Cappellitani Scalzati, which is long and usually very busy. To-day, though, it's strangely smooth. Past the post office, I see a couple of pedestrians approaching the crosswalk. I manage to pass before them without any issues. I zoom past them. Out of the corner of my eye, I see them step back. I didn't do anything wrong, they hadn't started crossing yet. I'm in a rush! I have to go to the lawyer for the ownership of a 2-square-meter storage shed in Val Camonica, inherited from Aunt Drusebia... not ex-actly a walk in the park, right? There are more pedestrians up ahead and... wouldn't you know it, the Good Samaritan! The man driving the car ahead of me wants to atone for his sins and earn a plenary indulgence, so he brakes to let them cross. But darn it, they're so slow! I honk the horn and see the driver in front pointing at them. Finally, they take their first step. Damn it, I'm losing a lot of time! I have a serious appointment, not like you guys! I swerve to the left and start to pass the car ahead of me when I realize two kids holding hands are emerging from be-hind the front hood. What the hell! And where are the parents? I slam on the brakes, tires screeching, skidding. The car stops just in time a few meters from the children. I angrily gesture for them to hurry across. To the right, the Samaritan driver mocks me sarcastically. I motion for him to mind his own business. Af-ter the two little ones pass, the pedestrians from before are also crossing, and I'm forced to wait for them too. I have an appoint-ment, got it? Sure, you're supposed to stop at pedestrian cross-ings, but you're also supposed to walk quickly, you know?

11 Car accident [A]

Amelia, 6:45 PM on any given day

I'm heading back home and I'm really tired. Today's workday has been terrible, I can't believe it's finally over. I drive towards Alfaratani Street. After the main road, I'll finally be home. Here comes the dreaded stop sign that I face every day. I pause for a fraction of a second, well, not really a pause, just rolling slowly. I inch out and BAM, an idiot coming from the left hits me head-on. I get out of the car, a bit dazed, not knowing what to say or do. I start to say something accusing, but then the furious guy getting out of the other car points out clearly that I didn't stop at the stop sign. I fall silent without protesting. Yes, because in an instant I realize he's... right, damn it, he's absolutely right. So I look at my car, not much damage... and then I look at his, the right headlight is smashed along with part of the bumper. Well, at least the insurance won't have to pay millions of euros. We exchange details, he massages his neck. I hope it's just whiplash but... no. At some point he says he'll have to go to the emergency room for a quick check-up due to neck pain. I tell him it couldn't have been the accident, it happened at a very low speed, at an angle that couldn't have caused whiplash! But no... he says it's his call what he does. He says goodbye and walks away. Okay, I may have made a small mistake, but he had plenty of time to brake. A fraudster at heart! He hasn't suffered a thing, besides, being as big and hefty as he is, that bump probably tickled him, like it did to me. A few days later, the insurance informs me of the damage: 1500 euros to repair his car and... 3500 euros for the bodily injury. Can they be any more dishonest than this?

Car accident [B]

Amelia, 7:10 AM on another random day

I'm stuck in traffic like every damn morning on the avenue packed with cars, moving at a snail's pace that seems to stretch for tens of kilometers, though in reality it's no more than 400 meters. We move in waves, as usual when there's a jam. Every now and then yeeees, we're moviiing... then screeeech. Everyone brakes suddenly. I keep a safe distance from the car in front of me. I absolutely don't want to make the mistake of going too fast and not being able to stop BAAAM. What happens? Suddenly everything jolts around me, and so do I. A sharp, violent impact at the rear of my car. I look in the mirror and see a girl, already raising her hands to apologize. Did you rear-end me? Now you're in trouble, sweetheart! I get out, furious, and inspect the rear of my car. All in all, nothing serious, but the trunk is jammed! How will I get my backpack and computer out? Damn it, besides wrecking my car, you've ruined my day. I vent my anger at her, curse the lack of respect for safe distance, her driving incompetence, her carelessness. She's mortified, apologizing repeatedly. I calm down. Anyway, she's completely at fault, that's what the traffic code says. Fortunately, I didn't rear-end anyone in front of me. We exchange insurance details for the damage report, she signs it. I just want to fix my car, nothing more. Should I go to the office? No, I'm a bit shaken, I'll go home, no... I'm not stupid! I'll go to the emergency room and get a nice whiplash diagnosis. It's not fair that I always end up being the stupid one who suffers. And I really felt the impact! Who knows if my vertebrae haven't suffered some damage? You've ruined my day, wrecked my car, and probably caused me physical harm. Now I'll show you who I am, little girl!

12 Alcohol ^A

Bastiano, 1:00 PM on any given day

Here's yet another news report on TV telling of a fatal accident involving vehicles driven by motorists who had consumed alcohol before getting behind the wheel. How can people be so stupid, so reckless, so irresponsible? Even if they are fortunate (fortunate?) enough to survive, they've still ruined their lives because carrying the guilt of another person's death leaves no escape. And all for what? For trusting too much in their driving skills, in their alcohol tolerance, as if rules weren't important, as if the law made no sense, as if it hadn't been written by people who studied the effects of alcohol perfectly on our ability to concentrate. And now, another family mourns their children who will never come home again because of the stupidity of their peer. The deceased, innocent, pay with their lives for the foolishness, idiocy, and recklessness of an idiot who has destroyed everything, his and their lives, due to supreme stupidity, due to overconfidence. And then, I realize that you might not understand the damage that particular cocktail has caused you, I get it that without a breathalyzer you don't know if you're capable of driving or not, but at least avoid driving like an idiot! You're not even a toenail of a race car driver and racing cars are much safer than those on the road, do you understand? Avoid increasing the risks that normally exist when drinking. And no, you were going 90 km/h in the city and didn't slow down at any intersection. Yes, because on one hand alcohol progressively reduces attention span, slows reflexes, on the other hand it removes inhibitions, reduces the fear sensation that normally protects us from crossing the limits. I would have preferred if only you had died, at least you are guilty.

Alcohol [B]

Bastiano, 1:30 AM on another random day

I had a wonderful evening with my longtime friends. Now I'm heading home alone. I know, you shouldn't drive after drinking, but I handle alcohol perfectly well. I'm used to it, what harm could three 0.50cl beers possibly do? Beers are much lighter than wine, so even if you drink more, the alcohol concentration is so low that one of them, typically alcoholic, doesn't equate to even a single small glass of wine. Okay, they were 7% stout beers, but I drank them slowly, with food. I had plenty of time to digest them and neutralize the alcohol effect. I'm almost certain that if I took a breathalyzer test now, it would be negative. I handle alcohol better than almost all my friends who seem drunk after just a small glass of liqueur! When I hear about a traffic accident on the news where the driver had a high blood alcohol level, I think it's absurd to drive in those conditions. But deep down, I also feel that if it were me driving with an even higher alcohol level, I certainly wouldn't have been involved in the accident. There are really so many factors that contribute to how alcohol affects the body of a driver. The bloodstream in your circulatory system counts a lot! The more blood you have, the less effect it has on your ability to drive, right? I'm 1.84 meters tall, all that beer tickles me, seriously! I don't feel any negative physical effects, just a slight euphoria. And this is proof that alcohol has affected me very little, because euphoria is what you feel at the beginning when you start drinking. And that slight euphoria makes my journey home very pleasant. I push the pedal a bit, so I can get home a bit earlier. The streets are completely empty at this hour...

13 Parking and protected categories [A]

Clelia, 12:30 PM on any given day

My little ones will be born in 2 months, and I already look like a fully inflated balloon ready to burst at any moment. Nevertheless, I manage to handle various tasks besides going to the office. Moreover, thanks to parking spaces reserved for protected categories like disabled individuals and pregnant women, and with the help of carts that can be taken to the car, lifting little weight at a time, even family shopping is within my reach. Fortunately, these small yet essential conveniences exist for people in my condition. Sometimes I feel unjustly privileged, but ultimately my condition is indeed delicate, and I dismiss this silly thought in an instant. And then I see that people are kind to me when they realize I'm carrying two lives within me. And that makes me happy. Here we go... as expected. The 3 reserved spots in the supermarket parking lot for expecting mothers are all taken, along with all the other regular spots. The reason is clear... it's peak hour. Alright, no problem, I'll wait a bit, I'm not in a hurry today anyway. After 5 minutes, a man gets out of a car and approaches one of the 3 cars, opening it. Maybe his wife will follow him... no. The man starts reversing. I look closely at the dashboard looking for the disability symbol. Nothing. I get quite irritated. His window is open, so I lower mine and point out to him that he has occupied one of the 3 reserved spots. He responds very rudely, asking me why it should matter to me. I tell him I'm pregnant. He laughs and says his wife is pregnant too. I ask him where his wife is, and he says she's at home, then drives off laughing and squealing his tires!!! Rude, disrespectful, chauvinistic, fake, and a liar! I hope your wife is better than you!

Parking and protected categories [B]

Clelia, 10:00 AM on another random day

I have just dropped off Luigietto and Anacleta at their friends' place in a condominium with a courtyard where they can play freely, always supervised by their friends' parents. I have many errands to run, including grocery shopping. And I'm in a hurry because I have to be at my meditation guru's place by 10:45. It's the only time entirely dedicated to myself throughout the entire week. The supermarket's indoor parking lot is packed as usual. I circle around a couple of times, but it's all full. I'll have to take the car back up and find street parking, wasting even more time. Unless... well, yeah, come on, I'll be super quick, no one will notice. I take another lap and nose my car into one of the three parking spots reserved for protected categories. I used to be part of that category a few years ago, not anymore, or maybe I still am? Maybe people with small children still qualify? I dismiss this doubt because there are two other spots currently free, I won't harm anyone. I go up, do the shopping, and in just 20 minutes, I'm back down. And there, a disabled person has been honking for some time at my car. I apologize, and he gets angry, telling me those spots are reserved. I point out to him that there are two other free spots. He responds that he needs the one on the side because it's the only one that allows him to independently get into his wheelchair by unloading it from the rear seat. I tell him I was away for less than 5 minutes, and he says his time is precious too. But really! I respect you, brother, but I have a hectic day and very little time. I didn't harm you, and you still have a way to park. What the hell do you want from me today? You won't make me feel guilty, in fact, you're a bit rude. What do you think, being disabled gives you the right to walk all over me?

14 Used cars [A]

Bartolo, 10:30 AM on any given day

I'm about to buy a second-hand car. It's very cheap, despite having been lightly used, and that's very, very strange. Adding to that, the odometer shows only 45,000 kilometers driven, which makes it even stranger. But the car is really nice, really beautiful, and it's exactly the make and model I've been dreaming of. However, I won't be taken advantage of. I'm an honest person, but not stupid. The world is full of people who sell cars at the first sign of a technical problem that would require significant expenses to fix. Unscrupulous people who wouldn't hesitate to cheat someone just to get rid of a vehicle on the brink of collapse. I've never done that and I never will, but I know that fraud is just around the corner and I need to protect myself somehow. I don't think the dealer could be aware of it, otherwise they would never have taken the car to sell it. If there are issues, they are generally subtle, hidden, rarely evident even to the most rigorous inspections. So, if someone sold a car with a malfunctioning gamma disassembler, which only shows its malfunction once every 100 days, the dealer wouldn't know. But I'm very clever and before buying the car, I'll have it checked by two of my trusted mechanics. One is older, more traditional, but with vast experience who will test, feel, and examine it to determine if it's worth it or not; the other is younger, but highly technologically advanced, who will connect it to his computer and read every obscure detail about its past life, uncovering even hidden or erased information. I wasn't born yesterday, I'll only buy the car if it turns out to be in perfect condition!

Used cars [B]

Bartolo, 10:30 AM on another random day

My Bontari GLS now has 325,000 kilometers on it and its electronic control unit has started to give problems. I've already had it repaired twice and I'm at risk of getting into the classic cycle of continuous repairs that end up costing more than buying a new car. And you never know when to stop! So, I'm not sure what to do. Upon the third occurrence of the problem, I turn once again to my trusted mechanic for advice. He, succinctly, tells me that once the control unit starts having issues, it won't stop. Granted, these issues are infrequent, occurring once every 3,000 or 4,000 kilometers, but they exist and could leave you stranded in the middle of a journey. He suggests, in essence, that it's better to move on and think about a new vehicle. I ask him what I should do with my old vehicle. He mentions that I could use it as a scrappage vehicle, which would save me about €1,500 on the purchase of a new car, but I could also earn a little more... I ask him to specify how. He goes on to say that, with a 'makeover' at the body shop, a 'rollback' of the mileage to no more than 65,000 kilometers on the odometer, and a quick tune-up of the engine to delay the recurrence of the sensor problem as much as possible, without mentioning a word about it to any future buyer, he might be able to sell it for €3,000 – €3,500. Subtracting about €500 for the restoration work listed so far. Well, scrapping it would save me €1,500, but this option could save me at least €2,500. There's not much to think about, right? I immediately decide to take this opportunity. My car is strong, it has covered many kilometers and can cover many more. Plus, the problem might not occur again!

Gamification 2/10

Paragraph	Only A OR B	Both A AND B
3 Right of way	☐ 0 points	☐ 1 point
4 The traffic light	☐ 0 points	☐ 1 point
5 Speed limits	☐ 0 points	☐ 1 point
6 Driving and smartphones	☐ 0 points	☐ 1 point
7 The accelerator	☐ 0 points	☐ 1 point
8 Emergency lanes	☐ 0 points	☐ 1 point
9 Thunderstorms	☐ 0 points	☐ 1 point
10 Crosswalks	☐ 0 points	☐ 1 point
11 Car accident	☐ 0 points	☐ 1 point
12 Alcohol	☐ 0 points	☐ 1 point
13 Parking and protected categories	☐ 0 points	☐ 1 point
14 Used cars	☐ 0 points	☐ 1 point
TOTAL		

Religion and devotion

The more I study religions, the more I am convinced that man has never done anything but worship himself.

Richard Burton

15 Worship and freedom [A]

Aurora, 11:00 AM on any given day

I am going to withdraw some cash from my bank's ATM. I park and... uff, there's a bit of a queue, I'll have to wait. Right in front of me is a woman with beautiful eyes and face, framed, however, in a black veil... I think it's called a *hijab*. Instinctively, I feel annoyed by that restriction of freedom. Okay... she would probably tell me that it's her free choice and not imposed by anyone, but I still consider these rituals of other religions that limit individual freedom, especially if female, to be strange and damaging to freedom. I often hear news on TV about what they call *Islamic fundamentalism* and the issue of veils for women. This makes me think that maybe some wear it by choice, but not all really have the freedom to decide. And even if they choose to, I wonder what kind of religion with any respect for the individual would require this type of clothing. I'm quite drastic on this; I can't believe in free and individual choice. It's absurd to have to cover and, by doing so, mortify one's body just because the dogmas of your faith dictate it or even just because your overly religious man considers it a terrible affront not to! We're talking about something from the past, from a patriarchal past, of a religion that never updates itself. Not to mention the more extreme forms of this prehistoric custom, like the *burqa* or something similar. To me, a Muslim woman wearing the hijab is someone whose freedom has been absolutely limited. I look at my beautiful queue neighbor and while on one hand I sympathize with her as a woman, on the other, I want to scold her for her failure to rebel against this senseless custom, unfortunately still widespread today.

Worship and freedom [B]

Aurora, 7:00 PM on another random day

Today, I am participating as an organist in a meeting of various orders of nuns. The meeting is taking place at my parish, where I am very active and involved in various activities. Here they come, all together, with their classic outfits, the habit, and their wonderful, white veil on their heads. Today they are in their ordinary dress, where the face is surrounded by a narrower white veil. They are really beautiful, and I find their clothing very appropriate for their mission. It is nice that there are still orders like these, which make the respect for tradition one of their strengths. It is like having certainties that never leave you. The Catholic religion has always had troops of peace, people who choose to dedicate their lives to others. Secular and habited nuns, missionaries, friars, priests. All with their attire, all with their order and rules. And these nuns are part of that army! Their dress is really complex. Once, my friend Sister Pirulina explained to me the parts that make it up. First, there is the long habit that should not be tailored to the body to avoid highlighting female shapes, with long, wide sleeves and a belt at the waist. Then, on top, there is the *wimple*, which tightly wraps the neck and face and hides the hair. Then there is the *bandeau*, which covers the forehead, and on top of that is the veil that again covers the entire upper part. Some people want to insinuate that this is still a restriction of freedom! Come on, what nonsense! These women have freely chosen to be active members of the religious hierarchy, wearing millennia-old traditional clothing by choice and not by imposition! They can leave the vows whenever they want! The comparison does not hold up at all. Nuns are brides of Christ, and they are beautiful as they are. Let's not talk heresies!

16 Rites and Sacred Books [A]

Bartolomeo, 6:30 PM on any given day

I am a very religious person. For me, the Catholic faith is the foundation of life and its rites are its pillars. It's not just tradition, for heaven's sake, or at least not only that. Every day after work, I leave home and go to the parish across the street where I happily spend much of my free time. Mass is fundamental, and I am participating in it today as well. The liturgical celebration, with its words, music, chants, and attire, revolves around the incredible gift that God has given us. He gave his life for us. Not in words, but in deeds. He died and rose again for us. And the day before he died, he also gave us the opportunity to forever repeat this pivotal moment. Every day, in fact, during the Eucharistic celebration, at the moment of consecration, an extraordinary physical transformation occurs in what the priest is blessing on the altar. *Transubstantiation*, a dogma of the Catholic Church, clearly tells us that the blessed bread truly becomes the flesh of the Lord and the wine truly becomes his blood. Not symbols, but truly flesh and blood. And we also partake in the divine banquet by consuming it, because God offers us his body! And then there are the key moments of the liturgical year that are precious to me. Moments that mark each year with the life of the Lord and its fundamental stages culminating in his death and resurrection. Resurrection that we too will live, if in life, we have sown as he teaches us. Christmas, Easter, these are moments to be lived with absolute devotion, in liturgy and in daily life, becoming more and more united with one's faith, with the word, with the Lord. The rites of the Catholic Church are fundamental for every good Christian. Participating in them with unquenchable faith and devotion is a source of absolute joy!

Rites and Sacred Books [B]

Bartolomeo, 6:30 PM on another random day

It's Saturday afternoon, and after a truly substantial and tasty lunch, I'm flipping through TV channels in search of something interesting. I don't want to watch movies or start a 12-season series that I'll never finish. Maybe a documentary. There it is! Religious rituals around the world. Let's see... voodoo? Hmm, incomprehensible rituals where members of some tribes gather in a circle semi-nude, while some play improvised drums on hollow logs with huge wooden sticks, and others dance and sing. What's the purpose of all this? And then, what about the *shaman* dressed like a colorful puppet, esteemed and revered for powers he doesn't have? Do they really believe they enter a kind of spiritual trance during these moments and can communicate with the world of the dead! Can you imagine? Communicating with the dead! The documentary continues, talking about an Indian sect whose followers consume human flesh! Fortunately, it's from corpses. They roam among funeral pyres on their sacred river, searching for parts of corpses to eat. How can this be? They may be dead, but it's still cannibalism! And there are many other rituals crazier than these that I don't even want to mention. It's incredible to see how far humans can go in the madness of their fanaticisms. Furthermore... on other continents, there are tribes where the purification of youths involves removing some of their blood through tubes inserted into their mouths. I am shocked by how easily humans believe in things like these. To think that such a ritual could somehow appease their imagined god who exists only in their minds. But then, what kind of god would ever require people to consume human flesh, whether alive or dead? Poor souls... lost in the rituals of religions based on foolish beliefs and inhumane acts.

17 Coherence [A]

Angelica, 12:30 PM on any given day

I am very religious and strive to uphold all the teachings that my Lord has given us. But I believe that we cannot stop at words alone; it is necessary to bring them into daily life. Consistency and adherence to doctrine should not be mere displays of pride to others, nor should we exhibit acts of *pharisaic* memory. Rather, we must truly live out what it means to belong to our faith. A Christian is a Christian only if they put into practice the teachings of the Gospel. Listening to the word of God is essential for every good Christian. I trust in my God and believe in His teachings. Among the most important teachings of my religion is love for one's neighbor, which should be loved as we love ourselves. It is something incredibly profound. Love, generosity, hospitality... they must always be at the center of our daily lives. Therefore, we must restrain our own cumbersome ego, stop being self-centered, and reach out to our neighbor. And by this term, I do not mean only our loved ones, family, or friends, but everyone we encounter along our path. The other person is our wealth, regardless of whether they can reciprocate our efforts. Love must be strong, selfless, and generous! It is startling to read the sacred book; its disarmingly simple language makes it relevant despite the centuries that have passed since it was written. One could read it even without being religious, and it would still remain a book of common sense because what it teaches is immediate, easy to understand, requires no special skills, and does not necessitate advanced studies. It simply says to love your neighbor as yourself! That's all.

Coherence [B]

Angelica, 11:30 AM on another random day

I detest my colleague who flirts shamelessly with the boss; I wish she were dead! I can't stand the fact that she tries to butter him up in every possible way, even in the most embarrassing ways. And that idiot falls for it. It's so obvious that the tactics she uses have the effect she hopes for. Truly absurd! And then there are all those suck-ups who are halfway between them, all unscrupulous climbers. I know well what they're up to at work, and as soon as I can, I'll spill everything to him. But now what...? Oh my goodness, another message from that idiot neighbor. How dare he write to me when I'm at work? What does he want? That I park wherever he wants just because he can't maneuver his bulky SUV? He should go to hell; there are reasonable demands and others less so. I don't have time, I'm at work. He can figure it out himself; I certainly can't come home just because he can't get through. This afternoon I have to leave a bit early because I have a medical appointment at the hospital. Incredible, right? Booked just two days ago with the national health service, and I can already have it despite waiting lists supposedly stretching for years. But no, they haven't cleared out; all it took was a call to a friend who's very obliging, and in a few hours, I had the appointment! In the end, mine might be a serious issue, although of course I hope not. Certainly not like all those appointments people make just for regular check-ups. There must be some priority, right? Well, I just respected it. Maybe they'll admit me for a few days for observation; I hope not in one of those rooms with 8 people. In that case, I'll call my old schoolmate Pirofono, who would surely arrange a room with a maximum of 2 people, certainly more decent than those others...

18 Sexual freedom – I [A]

Calogero, 5:00 PM on any given day

Like many others, I am deeply religious, but above all, I have a very high concept of God that, in my opinion, transcends a simple reading of sacred texts. Certainly, I have understood that my God, the God who made me, the God who created the universe, is pure love. He is the one who 'designed' me and brought me into the world. His plan for me was born millions of years ago. He created me out of pure goodness and loves me, regardless of how I am, my preferences, or my choices. He loves me sincerely, completely, magnificently, tirelessly! No, he is not the jealous and vengeful God that religious people of the past thought of; he is a gentle God who loves his creatures endlessly and desires to be loved in return by them, of course. My God is the creator, the giver of life. Let's take a moment to think about it! He gave us life by bringing us into the world and at the same time gave us his life in the greatest way imaginable! No God before him has sacrificed as much as he did, giving up his own son to save us. It is a sacrifice of the highest level, which produces immense pain and joy. My God is eternal goodness; he loves all his children indiscriminately. My God has no prejudices; for him, everyone is equal. My God is magnanimous, an example to emulate to overcome all pettiness. My God is above all evil and pettiness. He surpasses all my mediocrity, all my mistakes, and forgives. Actually, he doesn't even need to forgive because he is utmost goodness. It is I, at most, who, recognizing my mistakes, ask him for forgiveness for having hurt him, but at that moment, he has already forgiven me. There can be no doubt about God; his love is so great and perfect that there are no ifs or buts, no disputes or inaccuracies. His love is free from imperfections.

Sexual freedom – I [B]

Calogero, 9:00 PM on another random day

The news once again covered the latest attempt by a certain political faction to pass laws granting same-sex couples the same rights as heterosexual couples, even to adopt children! What a crazy folly. It's nonsensical from every perspective. Let's start with rights. Thankfully, in our country, it's not possible for same-sex couples to marry. Even if a marriage were conducted or recognized by a mayor seeking publicity, it wouldn't hold any legal value comparable to heterosexual marriage. And what about adoption? Can you believe it? I don't have adopted children, nor have I been adopted, but it's not difficult to imagine the impossibility of raising normal, healthy children in a family unit without a male or female parental figure! I don't aim to delve into such a vast topic, as I lack the expertise, but anyone can easily assert that children would grow up... differently! Let's move on to religion. If all major religions have always condemned homosexuality, there must be a reason, right? Popes, bishops, documents, books have all condemned these practices, which have nothing to do with God and the concept of family He created. Fortunately, they have also included in the catechism the observation that homosexual men and women do not respect the natural order established by God and should be considered a 'moral impurity'. Even when individuals are evidently homosexual from birth, they still have the opportunity to avoid their moral error through appropriate choices that do not necessarily translate their impulses into actual acts. Homosexual acts are always considered sinful.

19 Charity and the 'neighbor' [A]

Beatrice, 6:30 PM on any given day

I am convinced that it's not always necessary to attend religious rituals, as long as one adheres to the teachings of their own god. Listening to, reading, and especially meditating on His word, the word written by prophets and evangelists through Him, is more than enough to stay upright. I firmly believe that forgiveness, peace, acceptance, and charity cannot be mere words spoken without a life that reflects their essence. It takes much more than that! They must pervade every moment of the day, so that each of us can be... the salt of the earth. "Love your neighbor as yourself" is the most important of commandments. It's incredible how much love is in just one sentence. Do you know what this means? It means that I must always reach out to others, placing them at the center of my universe, caring for their needs, ensuring they are well, that they do not suffer in silence, that they have what they need to nourish body and soul. Exactly as our God has done for us. The greatness of this commandment is what makes our religion different from all others. A religion where there is a God who, instead of sitting on a heavenly throne amid splendorous decorations and adoring servants, descended to the same earth we tread upon, became the son of man, and then reached the ultimate sacrifice: dying for us. Killed by ignorance, prejudice, misunderstanding, pharisaism, and the selfishness of us human beings... And what did He do next? Did He finally use the prerogatives of a God to... seek revenge? No! He rose from the dead to forgive those who had killed Him, thus teaching us a supreme love, unconditional and without reservation. We must bring that love into our lives and offer it to our neighbor. Just as the Samaritan did on the road he was traveling. Loving the poor, the hungry, the destitute... that is the way!

Charity and the 'neighbor' [B]

Beatrice, 11:30 AM on another random day

What a bunch of riffraff gathers near the central station of my city! I just got off the train and I'm greeted by rows of homeless people piled up on the ground with their filthy makeshift blankets. Every now and then I see an eye flicker among that filth and I wonder how anyone can live in such conditions, but especially how they can end up there in a city that is, so to speak, civilized. And here's one standing up, begging, asking me for some change. It's mid-morning and he's already completely drunk, the stench of alcohol can be smelled from several meters away. I quicken my pace and shake my head to let him know I have nothing to give him. I certainly don't want to fill his pockets with my money, which would surely end up in another bottle of wine. What a life! Doing nothing from morning till night every day of the week, waking up late, begging money from passers-by, probably accumulating piles of cash that wouldn't surprise me if they far exceeded my hard-earned salary. I pass the usual group of immigrants huddled on their sidewalk and without even lifting my head, I feel their eyes analyzing me as if I were prey, which I probably am. Again, I quicken my pace and cross the street. And there's the usual old wrinkled lady, pushing her shopping cart, stolen from some supermarket, filled with bags containing maybe her stuff or who knows, perhaps the loot from some theft. I hire a car and head to the outskirts... and there are the usual women on the roadside, selling their bodies as if it were nothing. Is this my city?! Where is the security? Where is the tranquility? Okay, maybe they are less fortunate than me, but do they all have to live in this city? There must surely be other places more suitable for them. I wish they would disappear instantly, I can't stand them at all. And I'm afraid of them...

20 The Golden Calf and the Saints [A]

Casimiro, 9:00 AM on any given day

In these days, I have often reflected on two readings from sacred texts, concerning two particular episodes in particular. I remember some passages: "While he was on the mountain speaking with God and receiving the commandments, his people, believing he would not return, asked his deputy to make a god for them to worship. So he took their jewels and fashioned a *golden calf,* and they worshipped it. Their God saw this and said, 'They have quickly turned aside from the way that I commanded them! Now let my anger burn against them and destroy them!' But the leader pleaded with God to spare his people and forgive them, and God relented from his intended punishment. Later, the leader descended from the mountain, but upon seeing the golden calf, he became furious, threw down the tablets of the commandments, breaking them, and harshly rebuked the deputy and all the others. Then he burned the calf in the fire, ground it into powder, scattered it on the water, and made the Israelites drink it." And then the old book repeats things like this several times: "You shall not make for yourself an idol, or any likeness of what is in heaven above or on the earth beneath or in the waters under the earth. You shall not worship them or serve them; for I, the Lord your God, am a jealous God." What is the evident meaning of all this? Absolutely, one must not create idols of silver or golden images! Another passage that struck me is the role of the precursor, who cries out in the wilderness that another man will come, our God, who will save us, and for whom we must straighten the paths and prepare the way. But the precursor tells everyone not to compare themselves to God, and no one should worship him, because he is not God; God is someone else. I am fascinated by the greatness of this man who announces the coming but steps aside with great humility, as is right!

The Golden Calf and the Saints [B]

Casimiro, 7:30 PM on another random day

The new statue of the Son of God placed at the entrance of our place of worship is beautiful beyond words! Its towering presence instills a profound sense of reverence. Personally involved in its creation, we deliberated over materials and finishes, gathered generous offerings, and now, here it stands! Every passerby genuflects in its presence, deeply moved by its grandeur. Alongside the sacred paintings depicting the Stations of the Cross, it creates an atmosphere of profound mysticism and meditation. The artist behind this masterpiece is exceptionally skilled. To express our gratitude for our daughter's recovery from a serious illness, my wife and I have made a significant financial effort to commission a solid gold heart. This heartfelt offering will be placed alongside others in front of the portrait of the Lord's mother, housed in the renowned western sanctuary where millions of faithful visit annually. While there are many sanctuaries around the world where similar images are venerated, this one holds a special place in our hearts. In our own sanctuaries, paintings discovered in caves, wells, boats, and cellars are also revered, but this one holds particular significance. Thousands of faithful visit each year, feeling the tangible presence of God. The grace bestowed upon us through our daughter's recovery is priceless and serves as a testament to someone else's benevolence! Moreover, the neighborhood assembly has recently approved the installation of a statue honoring the highly revered Father Muo on the adjacent street. He is a pivotal mystical figure for us believers, marked with the signs of our God on his body and serving as a guiding light. We frequently visit his sanctuary, seeking his intercession for various challenges we face. There are numerous accounts of his miraculous interventions, supported by compelling evidence!

21 The foundations of faith ^A

Corrado, 12:00 PM on any given day

As always, I am attending Sunday Mass. Today is a special day for us believers because we celebrate one of the most important moments of the year. In my religion, there are truly unique aspects that require absolute faith. Indeed, faith is the foundation of my religion. Without faith, one cannot fully and peacefully live their commitment to the Lord because doubt, which plagues us, somehow represents evil. No, evil is not a horned little demon tempting you; no one believes that. The true evil lies in doubt. I strive to remain rational. Having faith doesn't mean believing in flying donkeys but accepting as true certain things fundamental to one's belief. The mother of my Lord conceived her son, God made flesh, begotten but not created, through a conception without physical contact. Perhaps it is the first of my God's miracles in the new sacred book. And my God became man but at the same time remains God. His mother is a human woman but also his true mother. At her death, she was assumed into heaven and now sits there with the Father and Son. My Lord gave himself to us in his greatest sacrifice, allowing himself to be killed to show us that there is no greater love than to lay down one's life for one's friends! And then he returned among the living and now sits beside his Father. With him and the Holy Spirit, the three are one. Yes, they are three persons, but they are also the same person. And the sacrifice of my Lord is fulfilled every day during the celebration. In it, the bread truly becomes flesh and the wine truly becomes blood. And then, beyond all this, there are the miracles recounted in the new sacred book. In this and much more, one must firmly believe. This is the essence of having faith. These are the foundations of my religion!

The foundations of faith ^B

Corrado, 10:30 PM on another random day

With my friend Dharma, we discuss the motivations underlying faith. He asserts that our sacred texts hold immeasurable value regardless of the Church's declarations in various councils over the years, statements not directly from God. He says our sacred book describes how every person should live, loving and respecting others. According to him, this does not depend on the supernatural or miraculous aspects throughout the history of our religion from day zero to today. He asks if I believe because what our God affirms is relevant or because he turned water into wine? Do I believe because his commandments are to be absolutely followed or because he healed a blind man or raised the dead? Do I believe because loving others as myself is a universally valuable commandment or because the mother of the incarnate Lord was a virgin? At times, he gets upset because he wonders, ultimately, why we should care about the otherworldly characteristics of these deities or their miraculous acts when what they preach is what truly matters. Indeed, in the stories of divine history, at least in the new books, the protagonists placed their superhuman qualities absolutely in the background, and if they revived a dead person, it was because they loved that person and did everything possible for them. Dharma finally says that for our God, the essence is to love, love, love. He argues that almost all dogmas were decided hundreds of years later by religious leaders who had to address the people's questions on various issues but did not come directly from the deities themselves. This is true, I admit, but I still believe it was my God who inspired those men to promulgate these rules. Faith is faith; it either exists or it does not.

22 Infallibility of the head of the church [A]

Carlotta, 11:00 AM on any given day

I am very religious and have faith in my God. As a religious person, it is essential for me to have a deep understanding of sacred texts. Not only those which are a historical transcription of the words of my incarnate Lord, but also and especially those that came after, written by religious figures inspired by God who, over the years, have strived to keep our religion relevant, capable of providing answers to God's people. The *doctrines* of my religion are many, among them is the infallibility of the head of the church. The head of the church is not there by chance; his election pleases our Lord. He is the successor of the one whom the Lord clearly considered the most important among his apostles. It is not coincidental, therefore, that a cardinal or another high-ranking prelate is elected to the pinnacle of my church. Only someone truly capable of lovingly and authoritatively guiding the Lord's flock can be invested with such an office. Furthermore, the head of the church is infallible. In what sense? The dogma of infallibility means that the head of the church, who is also the spiritual guide of all the faithful, is infallible not only when defining doctrine, the principles of our religion, but also and especially, for me, when defining the correct moral conduct of the faithful. The sacred books were written thousands of years ago and, although they remain highly relevant, they still require an authoritative interpretation that allows the values contained within them to be applied in everyday life, enabling the faithful to interpret daily events and make appropriate decisions in accordance with these teachings. The head of the church helps us through his speeches, his letters, his books, to live a moral life consistent with our religious beliefs and respectful of the will of our God.

Infallibility of the head of the church [B]

Carlotta, 6:00 AM on another ordinary day

Today the head of our church said some rather strange things. I don't relate to them at all, and unfortunately, it's not the first time this has happened. The current leader often expresses himself in ways that are not exactly conventional and make me think there's something wrong with his interpretations. They call him the progressive. But progressive in what sense? What kind of progress can there be in doctrine? I'm starting to fear him, I don't want to say hate, because he is the undisputed leader of the church, but when he makes statements so out of place and in which no one in our religion sees themselves reflected, I wonder what the difference is between him and... the Antichrist! I respect everyone... if someone wants to be with a person of the same sex, they are obviously free to do so, but for the head of my church to even say that those who judge homosexuality as wrong are themselves in error, well, that is not at all right. Perhaps the Lord does not love us for our sexual preferences, but because we are his children, regardless of our urges, yet the sacred book clearly elevates the traditional family composed of a man and a woman; any other type of family is, so to speak, unnatural. It also says that those who have sexual relations with someone outside of their marriage commit sin. Let me understand... so if I have a fling with someone and indulge in an affair, I've committed sin, but those who have relations with people of the same sex have not? The world is no longer as it should be; it's being subverted. And then there are many other things that I cannot tolerate, and he always dismisses them with the same phrase, "Who am I to judge?" But who are you indeed? You are the head of the church! You are the first to believe in the sacred books and should therefore know perfectly well what is good and what is evil!

Gamification 3/10

Paragraph	Only A OR B	Both A AND B
15 Worship and freedom	☐ 0 points	☐ 1 point
16 Rites and Sacred Books	☐ 0 points	☐ 1 point
17 Coherence	☐ 0 points	☐ 1 point
18 Sexual Freedom - I	☐ 0 points	☐ 1 point
19 Charity and the 'neighbor'	☐ 0 points	☐ 1 point
20 The Golden Calf and the Saints	☐ 0 points	☐ 1 point
21 The foundations of faith	☐ 0 points	☐ 1 point
22 Infallibility of the head of the church	☐ 0 points	☐ 1 point
TOTAL		

Ecology

Everyone constantly talks about wanting to return to nature, but no one wants to go there on foot.

Andrew J. Wollensky

23 Dirty streets (in the city) [A]

Dionisio, 7:50 AM on any given day

I'm driving on Via degli Pterodattili Redivivi towards my office. There's already the usual traffic of everyone heading to work like me. At a certain point, at the traffic light, the driver of the car in front of mine lowers his window and throws out the plastic and foil of a cigarette pack he had just opened, all with extreme indifference. The litter lands on the road and is run over by my car and then by all the others as the light turns green. I watch it flutter in the rearview mirror and am dumbfounded. I mean, seriously! Is it possible to act with such blatant disregard without thinking about the consequences? We all know how polluted, dirty, and filthy the streets of our cities are, and this gentleman, like surely many others, makes them even dirtier without the slightest embarrassment or shame. And the streets belong to him too! It's an act of extreme incivility that cannot be justified in any way. Ok, there aren't trash bins at arm's reach for every driver at traffic lights, but that doesn't give us the right to litter. Come on! And then we tell ourselves all these nice stories about the importance of protecting the environment and putting trash in the proper containers. It's disgusting to look at our streets, full of paper scraps, bags, and empty bottles, blown around by the wind. And it's all because of a few uncivilized people like this gentleman who, instead of keeping their trash in the car door pocket or wherever until they can dispose of it properly, are completely indifferent to the cleanliness and decorum of the city. The city is my home, the place where I live and work, but it's also his home and that of everyone like him. Well, what can I do? I really wish that one day, when this gentleman opens his window at home, someone would throw a bag of trash inside, just like in the movies!

Dirty streets (in the city) [B]

Dionisio, 11:00 AM on another ordinary day

We are on the highway, and my wife, my kids, and I are heading to the capital for a pleasant weekend getaway. We enjoy breaking away from the ordinary and going on a little trip from time to time. Suddenly, the little one throws up everything he ate a while ago at the service station where we had lunch. Damn! I adjust the rearview mirror and see the mess. These things happen with kids, of course, I know. The little one starts crying, completely covered in vomit. Even my wife, sitting next to him, got a bit dirty. I don't want to stop at a rest area; we just got back on the road. I tell my older son to open the glove compartment. He pulls out the wet wipes and hands them to my wife, who starts cleaning everything. She empties a supermarket bag to put the dirty wipes in. But, thinking about it... that bag is essential for the little one's dirty clothes! Where to put the used wipes? Come on, it's an emergency, we're in trouble, I don't want the car to stink, and the next service area is 34 km away... and besides, it's basically paper dirty with biodegradable material. Nothing polluting! Okay, the wipes say not to flush them, but that's surely for other reasons. They will dissolve in a few hours, maybe less. A rain shower would destroy them in seconds. I certainly don't want to put that stuff in the side pocket of the doors. It would smell bad for weeks... It's decided, we'll get rid of them. I take the trash and, after quickly checking the distance of the car behind us, I open the window and throw everything out. I've also had the little one pee in an empty plastic bottle and then leave it at the first rest area. What else could I have done? Keep the pee in the car?

24 Dirty roads (outside the city) ^A

Carola, 9:30 AM on any given day

I started early today, my long Saturday morning walk. By 5:30 AM, I was already on the road, and now, after 3 hours of brisk walking and nearly 17 km covered, I'm crossing one of the most beautiful country roads in the area where I have the good fortune to live. Unfortunately, not everything shines as it should. Every 15 or 20 meters, I come across trash, bags, leftovers, piles of plastic, broken appliances… everything, really. But how is this possible? How does all this stuff end up here? It certainly doesn't get here by itself. It's awful to see such naturally beautiful places, which should be almost pristine, literally defiled and dirtied by the incivility of individuals who, despite having countless disposal options, instead of using curbside collection or taking everything to the recycling center, prefer to dispose of their trash this way, leaving it wherever, destroying and polluting landscapes of rare beauty. The environment needs to be protected, but truly protected, not just with words! This destruction must be stopped! The level of neglect and extreme incivility that these actions represent is intolerable in a society that calls itself superior and claims to understand the fundamental importance of stopping pollution and initiating and supporting recyclable waste recovery processes. These plastic bottles, which probably no one will bother to remove, could still be here in several centuries! Do you realize that? Such a superficial and thoughtless act causes environmental damage for 200 or 300 years! And then, those dangerous construction waste, that pile of spoiled food with all the insects thriving on it. I am appalled. I don't know which of you has the habit of doing this, but you are dangerous to the planet. All of you, from the first to the last!

Dirty roads (outside the city) [B]

Carola, 11:30 AM on another ordinary day

Great-great-grandfather Teverico passed away, and after all the hassle of the inheritance, we received a small plot of land with a habitable building and a tool shed. I had a friend do an inspection, and he told me that the shed's roof is made of dangerous asbestos, which was widely used from the late 1800s to the 1980s. I immediately asked him what needed to be done, and he said there's a lengthy and expensive process for disposal. But seriously, is this an inheritance or what? I don't understand why I should bear the costs of disposing of something I didn't ask for. What fault is it of mine if my great-great-grandfather was born in an era when this type of material was widely allowed? If I have to spend a significant amount of money just to get rid of some waste, then this inheritance isn't really a great gift. We'll do it my way! I called some trusted friends and, with the proper personal protections, gloves, and masks, I had the roof dismantled. I loaded it onto a truck, and as soon as darkness fell, we transported the asbestos about 20 km away, leaving it on an unfrequented road. The garbage truck often passes by there, they'll notice it and send a specialized transport to retrieve it. It won't be a danger to passersby; after all, it's been here in the countryside for decades without causing any problems. I'll do the same with these old appliances because I have no way to take them to the recycling center. I still have this bag of smelly old clothes and food scraps. I don't know if I should take it with me... Come on, just this once... I'll leave it by the roadside... with everyone doing it, they'll have to come and pick it up sooner or later anyway. One more or one less... what difference does it make?

25 Water consumption (at home) [A]

Rodolfo, 12:30 AM on any given day

I hate waste, not just because of excessively high bills... I also despise it when it affects others' wallets. Particularly, I detest those who waste water. Such a precious resource thrown away without a second thought! Whenever I pass by my wife, my children, anyone with a tap left running, I always notice the amount of water flowing unused between tasks. For instance, I consider it a huge waste to leave the tap running full blast while brushing teeth. Come on! Why do that? While putting toothpaste on the brush, why let the water flow? And while rinsing the upper or lower arch of teeth? Sure, it's only a few seconds, but do you realize how many liters of water are wasted in those seconds over the course of days? Or when washing dishes. What's the point of keeping the tap at full blast from start to finish? Besides the annoyance of clean and dirty water splashing everywhere, why waste so much? Wouldn't it make more sense to wet everything, then shut off the water, remove the bulk with fingers or a sponge, and then rinse bit by bit? Or, if it must stay on, why not reduce the flow? The benefit isn't just financial; it's the entire planet that benefits! We need to realize there are many of us on this small globe, and resources are scarce for everyone. So, what you waste somehow goes into deficit for others. There are economic consequences too, because due to the scarcity of a precious resource like water, the costs for having it directly in our homes, clean and drinkable, keep rising... rightly so! Do you know how much effort goes into ensuring that water reaches you, drinkable, directly into your kitchen? And yet, we waste it!

Water consumption (outside the home) [B]

Rodolfo, 6:30 AM on another ordinary day

It's starting to cool down as autumn takes hold, inevitably moving towards winter. This morning I feel a bit chilly, and I don't like it at all. The house is still set up for summer, but I can quickly bring out a small fan heater to warm up the bathroom. It's crucial to me that the bathroom is warm and cozy. I hate freezing in there. Well, don't I deserve a little pampering like that? I wake up very early every day to ensure the whole family starts the day well. As soon as I enter the bathroom, I plug the bathtub and turn on the tap. I don't fill it completely, of course, because I don't have much time, but while I make coffee, it fills up about ten centimeters. That's enough for me to sit and even lie down, enjoying the warmth. And here I am turning on the tap. Damn it, the water is cold! I empty the tub and let the water run while keeping my fingers under the stream. Unfortunately, the bathroom is on the opposite side of the house from the boiler, so the water has to travel through the entire apartment before it gets here. After almost a minute, I feel the first warm stream on my fingers! Indeed, quite a bit of water is wasted during this phase, but I certainly can't take a bath with lukewarm or cold water, can I?! It's so pleasant to bask here, enjoying this wonderful warmth before starting the day. But all good things must come to an end, unfortunately, and I realize I'm running late... I pull the plug from the tub, get up, and with my feet still warm, I quickly shower to rinse off the soap. Maybe I'm overdoing it, I know, but I emphasize... I'm in a hurry! I can't be as careful as I'd like; work and school await all of us. And we certainly shouldn't skimp on personal hygiene, neither should my children and family. Okay, saving is important, but hygiene...

26 Water consumption (outside home) ^A

Penelope, 7:30 AM on any given day

Saving primary resources for the survival of the entire human race is absolutely crucial. Water, in particular, is an extremely precious resource for the survival of every living being, whether human, animal, or plant! Consider that a person can survive up to 30 days without food, but after just 4 days without water, they are destined for a rapid death. Water is essential; we are primarily composed of it. Water is life, but it can also be... death! Yes, because it can be a vehicle for serious diseases if consumed without proper purification. Just think, millions of people die every year because they are forced to drink contaminated water. Not everyone is fortunate enough to have water distributed through a reliable network without its purity being compromised by sewage infiltration, which must undergo extensive quality checks before reaching our faucets. The water we drink is sterilized multiple times before it ends up in the bottle on our table! That's why I value water conservation so much, and why everyone should be careful not to consume more than necessary. Water should be cherished. No one should waste it, and it's not difficult to find valid reasons to commit to this. It's enough to constantly think about the work, energy, effort, and care that were invested so that water could be immediately available when we open any of our faucets. And then, none of us deserve the world into which we were fortunate or unfortunate to be born. If you are born in one part of the world, having clean running water is such an obvious given that it's almost background noise. If you are born in another part, you may never see in your lifetime a faucet with clean, drinkable water. And you have no merit in this discrepancy!

Water consumption (outside home) [B]

Penelope, 7:00 AM on another ordinary day

My husband, our three children, and I are enjoying a wonderful vacation in the picturesque seaside town of Bagnèttolo. We've rented a cozy apartment perched right above the sea, complete with a lovely veranda where we can enjoy meals and relax in the cool sea breeze. Each day we choose our beach, with a preference for the more natural and secluded ones, even if they require a slow drive down narrow, unpaved roads. Our favorite beach, connected to the town by a winding path, demands careful driving to prevent damage to our car's suspension or the risk of a puncture. However, the stunning views and pristine environment make the journey well worth the effort! The dusty road kicks up a cloud of fine particles every time we traverse it, leaving our black car coated in a layer of dirt that gives it the appearance of an ancient relic upon our return in the afternoon. It's quite embarrassing to drive around like this, especially when we decide to venture into nearby villages for evening festivals and events. Fortunately, the owner of our apartment did not include water expenses in our rental agreement, allowing us the freedom to rinse off the accumulated dust from our car twice daily. Despite the cost considerations, we find it necessary to maintain our car's cleanliness, and the process has turned into an enjoyable activity for our children, who eagerly participate in washing off the dust amid the summer heat. While we are conscious of the cost implications, particularly given how others may perceive water usage, we justify our actions by recognizing the minimal impact of using a reasonable amount of water to rinse our car. With the abundant waste prevalent in daily life, using water for this purpose feels justified, especially as we strive to minimize our overall environmental footprint during our stay in this beautiful coastal paradise.

27 Waste separation [A]

Fabiano, 9:30 PM on any given day

I'm on my way to the nearest recycling center to dispose of several bags of waste. Environmental stewardship is deeply important to me, so I prioritize practices that conserve resources and respect the environment. I am meticulous about recycling. Here are the types of bags I have: glass, paper, organic, mixed, and plastic. Each material holds a different level of importance for me. Glass is fully recyclable and can be reused indefinitely. Paper, while recyclable, requires fresh cellulose to make new paper, making recycling crucial in reducing the need for deforestation. Organic waste can be turned into compost through proper composting methods. Challenges arise when it comes to plastic, with every household producing at least two bags per week, and mixed waste, which typically ends up in landfills. I am particularly sensitive to these latter issues and make every effort to avoid disposing of plastic in mixed waste or street bins, striving to minimize mixed waste by increasing the proportion of recyclable materials. Witnessing people casually discard plastic bottles into mixed waste bins prompts me to wonder why they don't take the minimal effort to place them in the nearest plastic recycling bin instead. There are various alternative solutions, such as installing waste-to-energy facilities and overlooking the amount of mixed waste remaining, as these large facilities autonomously sort, clean, and recover primary materials. However, I question whether installing them is truly beneficial considering their significant environmental impact. With a small effort, each of us can contribute to advancing the recycling process!

Waste separation [B]

Fabiano, 11:30 AM on another random day

I tried to have recycling bins installed in the office. At one point in my long career, I managed to get them installed, albeit only externally to the building and without any staff awareness campaign. So, I asked my closest colleagues in my area to split the cost and purchase at least two bins to keep in our room: one for paper and one for plastic. They happily agreed, and for years, we diligently collected and deposited recyclables into the external bins ourselves. However, the truth is that nobody wants recycling bins in the hallways or even multiple bins under their desks. They're considered unsightly and aesthetically unpleasing. What can I do? Now that I work on the 46th floor of a skyscraper in Megalopolis, I'm forced to throw everything in the trash because there's simply no other option. I can't take my plastic bottles or used paper reams and keep them aside in a bag to take out later. The same goes for organic waste... just the peel of a single fruit can create foul odors for days. Sure, I could go to another area of the office and use the recycling bin that's actually there, but I know perfectly well, and many colleagues have confirmed, that the cleaning company mixes everything and throws it all in the general waste anyway. And even if they didn't, it would be municipal sanitation workers who do it, so I throw everything in my bin and that's it. I'm sorry, but I don't see any alternatives. If I'm out on the street with colleagues and I have an empty plastic bottle in my hand and can't find recycling bins, I'll throw it in the first trash can on the corner. It's certainly not my bottle that's going to destroy the planet!

28 Flora and fauna [A]

Clarissa, 11:00 AM on any given day

I have always been socially active in defense of the natural environment, advocating passionately for the protection of flora and fauna. Nature must be respected unequivocally because it is our only home, at least until we successfully inhabit another planet, hopefully without destroying it. When you think about it, we can consider ourselves a species of exterminators, destroyers of natural habitats. Human intelligence surpasses that of other living beings, yet it is not great enough to understand that there will be no happy ending if we continue like this. The damage has already been done; urbanization completely destroys the previous ecosystem. That's why, wherever possible, we should protect what remains. A plant is no more or less worthy than us to inhabit this planet... it deserves to be safeguarded. A thousand-year-old tree cannot be cut down! It is a living being just like us and deserves respect and protection. Not to mention animals, which are much closer to us on the scale of consciousness and, like us, understand and experience emotions such as joy, fear, love, and the sense of family to varying degrees. Flora and fauna are not a theatrical backdrop to dismantle and replace with something better, simulating a semblance of life... they are life itself, the very expression of our planet. They are better than us because they respect nature; they do not destroy it. It's as if our intelligence has enabled us to surpass a limit that is still clear in flora and fauna: the world and its living beings are our world and our brothers and sisters; we must protect our cradle and everything that lives within it, alongside us.

Flora and fauna [B]

Clarissa, 7:30 PM on another random day

Unbelievable! I step out of the house to take the garbage to the recycling center, and as I approach, I see a wild boar eating from an open garbage bag on the asphalt. Hungry wild boars can be dangerous, and I'm alone. I turn around and start heading back, but then I look again at the animal that looks up at me. Now there are three of them! Two more hungry animals have appeared from behind the dumpsters. How am I supposed to know how hungry they are? I decide to go back home and throw the bag away tomorrow. I understand the importance of protecting animals in the name of nature, but enough is enough. It's not normal for me to fear an attack just stepping out of my house to take out the trash! Among wild boars, there's even competition for dominance within the herd. All that's missing is encountering a tough specimen kicking around to impress a mate, or a hungry mother devouring her less promising offspring. And all this is happening right outside my home! The reason for this hostile presence is surely linked to the nearby marsh, with its swamps and dense vegetation... a sort of small jungle created by the stagnation of a nearby natural stream. I don't understand why the municipality, aware of the problem, doesn't take action to clean up that area, which has become a haven for mosquitoes, rats, monstrous plants, and, indeed, wild boars. We're invaded by swarms of insects in summer and plagued by these uncontrollable animals all year round. The stagnant water emits a foul odor. Ideally, everything should be disinfested... bring in the bulldozers, remove the bend of the river and straighten it out to eliminate the marsh, clean up the muddy terrain, and perhaps create a nice playground for families and children, to create a usable public green space rather than leaving it as a dangerous and infected no-man's-land as it is now.

29 Infrastructures [A]

Fausto, 9:00 AM on any given day

I hear about infrastructure on the radio news and how our country is lagging behind in this phase. I really don't understand how this goal isn't clear to everyone. Nowadays, remaining competitive on a global economic level is crucial. Equally important is having citizens not burdened by countless bills, taxes, and the like, who can afford a good level of education and a dignified life. This country truly needs infrastructure… new, modern, advanced, and functional. I really don't understand those who make such a fuss opposing the construction of a 12km railway line! Thank goodness highways were built after the war; otherwise, today we wouldn't be able to build anything. We absolutely must evolve from our current state in terms of roads, bridges, connections, physical and digital networks, reaching the level of other global powers. We need to become independent in gas supplies, reduce the cost of transporting raw materials by installing new pipelines and any solution to save on the expensive transport of consumable goods by road. We must be able to face markets with strength, determination, and above all, the authority of knowing that behind us is a country that has managed to shake off inertia and equip itself to be a standard-bearer of modernity, simplification, and efficiency. At the same time, we must be a great country that facilitates and encourages the entry of foreign tourists eager to enjoy our wonderful valleys and mountains, our sea, and our vast artistic heritage. Foreign tourists should come to us knowing they will find a place fully capable of supporting their travel needs, accommodation, and more.

Infrastructures [B]

Fausto, 9:00 PM on another random day

I've just learned on social networks that the government wants to land the gas pipeline from the east in my region. And where? On one of our most beautiful beaches! The news has been confirmed by the most important national news broadcasts. Are we kidding? With all the places available, with nearly 1000 kilometers of coastline on this sea, they have to come and pollute right here? Yes, I understand it's the closest point to the other shore, but what would change if they landed it further away? They say it's crucial for the evolution of infrastructure. Okay, I get it, I'm an advocate for this modernization, but why do it right in my backyard? There are countless places, even less populated, less beautiful, less significant where it could be done. The project leaders have assured that nothing will harm the natural habitat and that the beach, after burial, will be as beautiful as, if not more beautiful than before. They also claim that the pipeline itself doesn't pollute. Maybe not, but the construction work, the machinery, the earth-moving, etc., that does pollute! I will join others in protest and take to the streets as I did when I was young to make my voice heard. We will protest against the luxury residence that some rich guy wants to build here, ignoring the environmental impact it could have on our ancestral lands. We have centuries-old trees that must be respected and protected at all costs. He guarantees that every uprooted tree will be replaced with young and strong trees, but we want our millennia-old trees. He has assured that he will transport the millennia-old trees elsewhere, but we do not want a single leaf to be harmed on these living beings. We do not want anything touched, and we want the environment that surrounds us to remain unchanged!

30 Vehicle maintenance [A]

Agnese, 10:30 AM on any given day

I'm in the office, overhearing my colleagues delve into discussions about cars and engines. Typically, I don't engage much with these topics that seem to captivate the guys, but today my attention is caught because my colleague is visibly concerned. She's noticed strange noises emanating from the engine of her utility vehicle and is eager to diagnose the issue before consulting a mechanic. The discussion among my colleagues, who are self-proclaimed experts in automotive mechanics today, spans several hypotheses. Initially, they speculate about potentially faulty timing belts, then shift to the possibility of scored cylinders, and finally consider whether the problem lies in a malfunctioning combustion chamber. The conversation leads to a pivotal concern: the anticipated cost. My colleague appears anxious, almost letting out a gasp when one of our colleagues suggests that repairing the cylinder head could exceed €1500. She visibly relaxes a bit when another colleague proposes an engine modification that promises to address all the issues. However, there's a catch... this modification is controversial because it's both theoretically illegal and environmentally harmful. It involves machining the cylinders to increase their capacity and replacing the pistons with larger ones. Despite the potential savings, about 33% less in cost, this alteration would fundamentally alter the car's engine specifications, increase its emissions, and potentially violate regulatory standards. I voiced my concerns about these legal and environmental implications, but one colleague dismissed them, humorously suggesting that once the engine is sealed, law enforcement would never notice any modifications. I'm left feeling bewildered by this casual attitude toward legality and environmental impact. It's truly perplexing...

Vehicle maintenance [B]

Agnese, 6:45 PM on another random day

I have a problem with my car. The loss of power I experienced on the way back from work is really concerning. I was in the middle of overtaking another vehicle when suddenly the accelerator stopped responding. Luckily, the car behind the one I was overtaking noticed my difficulty and helped me get back into my lane safely. I continued much more slowly and managed to return home. Before heading home, I visit my trusted mechanic. I trust him completely; he never seems to want to rip me off and always offers several possible solutions for me to choose from based on effectiveness and cost. Once he connects the car to an external analyzer, the generic fault light on the dashboard turns out to be related to a certain oxygen sensor that detects the percentage of oxygen in the exhaust gases, allowing the catalytic converter to do its job of reducing the car's polluting emissions. My sensor is completely shot! Unfortunately, it's not possible to replace just the sensor because it's welded in place by the factory. The entire exhaust system, from the engine to the rear pipe, needs to be replaced. The cost? Astronomical! €2500, including labor. I'm shocked by this estimate. I ask my mechanic if there are any other options. He hesitates and responds that yes, there are, but they involve disabling the sensor and removing the catalytic converter from the exhaust system. This will solve the problem, but my car will pollute like a vehicle from the 1920s. I ask him how much this alternative would cost, and he says it wouldn't be more than €120, including labor. I agree without hesitation. I can't afford to spend an entire salary just to turn off a warning light! Besides, I'm certainly not the one causing pollution; there are much, much more polluting vehicles than my little car.

31 Electric vehicles [A]

Fedele, 9:45 AM on any given day

I am deeply committed to the environment and believe that one of the ways to respect it is by becoming aware of one's ecological footprint and, where possible, minimizing activities harmful to the environment and polluting choices. One area where I feel I have made the right choice is in personal mobility. Recently, I purchased an electric car for my family. While I paid a bit more for it, it's truly worth it. Now, I can be certain that I am no longer contributing to urban pollution in any way. Additionally, I enjoy several benefits, including economic ones such as free parking in blue zones, hassle-free access to restricted traffic areas, and exemption from vehicle tax for several years. The greatest benefit? It may sound strange, but I feel it deeply within: my electric car is environmentally friendly. Traditional internal combustion engine vehicles use fossil fuels and are extremely harmful to the environment. To those who argue that electric cars are not truly environmentally friendly because the energy used to power them often comes from fossil fuels, I respond that I have taken care to choose wisely in this regard as well. I have opted for an electricity provider that charges a bit more but clearly states on my bill that a significant percentage of the electricity is generated from renewable sources! Moreover, they assure me that this percentage is set to increase over time, as the conversion of both national and international power plants progresses. Therefore, my car is not only environmentally friendly in its immediate environment; I am not creating a cleaner city at the expense of other places where the environmental impact of moving my car remains intolerable. Instead, for a good part of its life cycle, my car is environmentally friendly!

Electric vehicles [B]

Fedele, 12:15 PM on any other day

Today I received one of those generally detested phone calls during which, however, the operator made a truly interesting proposal. It was this that caught my attention just as I was about to hang up... He said that I would pay almost half the electricity bill. Intrigued by this, I decided to listen to him for a few minutes, taking a moment to isolate myself. Essentially, the proposal concerns the domestic supply of electricity. He told me that if I decided to switch to their service, I could have electricity at a cost that is practically half of what I currently pay, excluding taxes. Since I've had an electric car, I no longer spend money on fuel, but obviously the electricity bill has increased significantly. Every evening, I have to charge the car so that it's ready to cover the usual 130 kilometers I have to drive the next day. It really seems like there are no catches in this offer, except that it involves losing the percentage of energy produced from renewable sources. Yes, because ironically, in this transitional phase, the rise of renewables, and the popularity that comes with it, has led to a decrease in the price of energy derived from fossil fuels! It sounds strange, but ultimately it makes sense. He also encouraged me to take advantage of it without too many scruples because this offer won't last forever, precisely due to the ecological transition. Hmm... I accept. From now on, my ecological footprint won't be as pristine, but I certainly won't be the one destroying the planet. As the operator said, this energy has already been produced, so it doesn't make sense to waste it! I save quite a bit of money, and that was one of my goals when I bought the electric car. And besides, my car is one in a billion that pollutes more than 250,000 times mine every day over 10 years!

32 Ecology and consistency ^A

Concetta, 6:00 PM on any given day

Have you heard about the project to build a bridge connecting the mainland to one of our major islands? We're talking about an immense, titanic undertaking that, in my opinion, makes no sense at all! It's pure madness! I absolutely do not want them to build such a monstrous thing. It seems absurd to me to clear forests, construct, and drill through the marine environment just to allow cars to pass through when they have always used ferries! Those in favor argue that tourism will thrive, benefiting everyone, that goods will arrive faster, and that if we make such a fuss over this, we'll never have new infrastructure. There may be some truth to that, but we local residents are convinced that the ecological damage will far outweigh the benefits! Just today, I had a discussion with a colleague who supports the project. He says I should consider myself lucky to have the opportunity to travel on bridges, viaducts, and railway tunnels that were built when what he calls hypersensitivity to ecology didn't exist. He argues that if we were to stop everything today for what he considers trivial reasons, what would we have done after World War I when they began rebuilding the country? And what kind of country would we be if in the mid-1800s they hadn't started building the various Alpine tunnels that are still crucial today? I don't have a definitive stance on this, but I can provide an example. It's true that ecological awareness has evolved over the years, but it has changed for the better, to our benefit. One example is asbestos, which was widely used in construction until its danger was recognized, leading to its prohibition everywhere. The fact that in a certain historical period things once thought unthinkable could be done easily, and today they cannot, is part of the evolution in understanding the environmental value!

Ecology and consistency [B]

Concetta, 10:00 AM on another random day

I just stopped by my supermarket earlier, and they had colored bins on sale for household recycling: blue, yellow, black, and green. Alternatively, you could buy bags in different colors. Unfortunately, where I live, recycling isn't widely practiced, and the percentages are quite low... except in a few exemplary municipalities, let's say it's below 15%. This impacts citizens who have to make an effort to participate. What a hassle to repeatedly buy three different bags and ensure they're filled with the correct waste! Or even worse, to have four bins at home and end up keeping smelly stuff for a long time... No, no, I support ecology, but there's a limit to everything. Yesterday, I had guests over, and at one point, one of them, who had brought some preserves, asked me where the... compost bin was?! He assumed I had one since I have a small garden. I told him I didn't. Then he asked where the organic waste bin was, and I didn't know what to tell him because up to now, I've been putting everything in the general waste bin. Well, everyone contributes as they can. Let's think about positive things now. I'm going to lunch with a nice colleague today. I'm happy; we're good friends, and we haven't had a chat in a while. The restaurant is 300 meters from the office, but I don't feel like walking there. I'll take the car. Yes, it's true, the sun is shining, but it's lunch break, right? It's called a break for a reason. And besides, imagine the air conditioning! I would sweat quite a bit if I walked, and I don't want to feel uncomfortable all day with my blouse all wrinkled. I don't like no-iron shirts; they might be excellent in terms of keeping the crease, but they're not exactly top quality. Everyone knows it, even my colleagues who are always ready to gossip. It's better to avoid that...

33 Ecology and protest [A]

Flavio, 6:00 PM on any given day

Ecology is too important. It concerns the future of our planet and our children, grandchildren, and great-grandchildren. I want to do everything I can to protect nature. It's not about naive love for trees or animals, but a deep sense of responsibility toward humanity as a whole and the planet that hosts us. There are several issues that are close to my heart and should be to everyone's. One is the sustainability of everything we do, and another is pollution. Sustainability dictates that every use and consumption of resources, food, raw materials, should be accompanied by actions aimed at restoring them, so as not to create a definitive rift in humanity's future just because following the trend of crocodile handbags requires their extermination, or producing the latest powerful smartphone requires the extraction of a rare mineral found only in the state of Misereristan, where unfortunate people will kill each other to extract it for a few cents of their highly devalued currency, all so we can flaunt our jewel to friends and colleagues like crazy. Producing furniture from the famous Mobulusus brand requires so much wood that it clears half the Amazon rainforest! A forest that, as we learned in elementary school, is the lungs of the planet. Lungs that now suffer from diagnosed emphysema. But it seems that no one cares about this. Everyone wants to change the world for the better, but then no one does anything. Those who buy electric vehicles thinking they've made an eco-friendly choice, do they know that the energy produced for their operation still comes from fossil fuels? Do they know that the lithium batteries powering these fantastic vehicles are produced in distant countries, at the cost of immense pollution and unimaginable human exploitation?

Ecology and protest [B]

Flavio, 9:00 AM on another random day

Enough hesitation, ecology is a serious matter, so I've decided to take action! I'm participating in a protest organized in the capital of my state. It's a protest against our government... no, I mean, it's a protest against governments worldwide that do too little, far too little, for global ecology. This will be just the first of many days we'll organize to make ourselves heard, to shake the rubber wall on the other side, and finally get those in power to take concrete, impactful initiatives that can turn around this dangerously stagnant situation. Today, we challenged the inertia of those who govern us. With a blitz in the city center and buckets of colored paint, we covered the sculpture by Bernericio Madulerio, dedicated to honesty and erected right in front of the seats of power! Real paint, not the washable kind used by those who pretend to protest just to appear as heroes later on media and social platforms. Yes, we did it, we splattered this artwork with paint, and now incredulous and cowardly citizens are staring at us, insulting us, and all grabbing their phones. But we're slipping away now, not out of fear! Since we still have some paint left, we're running like crazy to reach other monuments in the area, in a city brimming with them. If nothing moves on the political front, here we are, making ourselves truly heard, protesting visibly against common indifference, against governmental inertia, against complacency with the status quo. We're not standing idly by, we're making ourselves truly heard! Here come the arrests now, okay, we'll pay for the damages, but our protest will have a significant impact, I'm sure of it. And maybe, finally, something will change.

34 Ecology and habits ᴬ

Corinna, 1:00 PM on any given day

Long live nature! I want it literally alive, not devastated by our wickedness. Long live the variety of species, habitats untouched by humans. I am fully supportive of protecting natural environments, ecosystems, and respecting global flora and fauna. I don't want to find myself on a planet where biodiversity has been compromised and the air has become unbreathable. Unfortunately, the planet is drifting, and it's truly difficult to halt environmental degradation. I believe the cause isn't solely in the hands of governments and politics, as certain protest movements occupying global squares would have us believe. It's not just a matter of national or financial interests. It's also, and above all, a personal issue! Because in the end, it's us who make the choices. Starting with those we delegate to manage public affairs: it's us who choose the politicians who will represent us. We're the ones who decide whether to consume meat from animals whose breeding harms the ecosystem. We're the ones who decide whether to consume a resource whose production is unsustainable... it's us! We make choices that are either polluting or environmentally friendly, opting for solutions harmful to the environment for immediate savings. Education in this regard, a culture of environmental respect, is essential to minimize the impact of personal choices on the natural environment. This should be taught to everyone, starting from a young age! Ecology shouldn't be just a vague concept as it has been so far, but a critically important subject with sufficient weekly hours in school curricula. It should be integrated into programs from elementary school through university, consistently emphasizing its importance.

Ecology and habits [B]

Corinna, 5:00 PM on another ordinary day

I'm so happy! I'm at the airport, in the private flight area. To-day, a very, very wealthy friend organized a ride for me on his private helicopter, and it was fantastic! We flew over our region, lingering over the most beautiful spots. As soon as he proposed it, I immediately accepted. I admit, I know perfectly well that a recreational trip on a polluting vehicle isn't exactly in line with my beliefs, but let's be honest... when will I get such an opportunity again? Besides, he probably would have taken the helicopter ride anyway, so I did the right thing by reducing the flight's footprint by increasing the number of passengers by one. And it doesn't end here... tonight, we'll dine at a Japanese restaurant where the food is divine! Of all the dishes, I prefer sashimi, and of all the varieties, I absolutely love fresh tuna; I eat a lot of it. I know that tuna fishing is one of the least sustainable human activities at the moment, probably because of the growing popularity of Japanese cuisine spreading rapidly around the planet, but what can I say, I'm crazy about it! It's not my little piece of tuna that's causing the problem, right? I face the same dilemma when we go to the best steakhouse in town. I know that meat production has a very high environmental impact, but I really love the taste of grilled meat too much to give it up. Again, do you think it's my consumption that's significantly increasing this problem? Even if I didn't consume or buy it, that meat would still have been produced, so what sense would it make to deprive myself? It's others who need to make changes in this regard, not me, who is just a small consumer like everyone else! I can do very little.

35 Organic food and beverages [A]

Fortunato, 8:45 AM on any ordinary day

Are we sure we live in an advanced society? And what is this belief based on? Excessive hygiene? Over-formalization of any legal act? The abundance of food? Besides, I'm not convinced these are real signs of civilization, let's focus on the food! I'm tired of overly refined and processed food, enough with preservatives, with chemicals, hooray for organic farming and livestock! It is absolutely not healthy to eat food and drink beverages that have undergone crazy treatments before reaching our table! Fruits and vegetables that have been sprayed, coated, submerged in substances like copper salts, sulfur (if you're lucky) and countless dangerous chemical mixtures (if you're not). And then what happens to this food? Sure, quite some time passes before these products reach our table, and the substances dilute a bit, but who guarantees that there are no residues? Who guarantees that there isn't a sufficient percentage left to harm me? In fact, it's certain that something remains, it's more than obvious! Maybe something that sneaks in... there, in tiny amounts and then, day by day, causes serious health problems like cancer or other issues! And then, do we want to talk about the selection of breeds, the modifications to DNA? Among all the treatments, the most unworthy and final one is genetic modifications to plants and animals... but does this seem normal to you? Does it seem healthy to consume this type of product? Do we have evidence of the potential harm that this violence against the natural order can cause? I don't want this type of product, I don't want to eat genetically modified vegetables, I don't want fruit whose genetic integrity has been violated, I want natural and organic stuff. I should have the right to decide what to eat!

Organic food and beverages [B]

Fortunato, 12:15 PM on another ordinary day

I produce organic wine thanks to the grapes from my ancestors' lands. I bottle quality wine! It's completely organic, with no treatments, except for those that are legal and within the scope of possibilities for products of this type. No additions of all those substances that make our wine harmful to health. You know when you buy a quality wine, drink three glasses, and don't feel excessively altered, while if you buy some cheap, non-organic wines that have undergone mysterious treatments, you get a headache from the third sip? Well, we can explain that ourselves. My wine isn't like that, my wine is pure! Inside, there is only fermented grape and a bit of sulfites in the quantities allowed by law. Sometimes I deviate a little, for example when the grapes are a bit old or the wine in the silos is already in an advanced fermentation stage. At that point, I stop the process with a slightly larger tablet than standard, but in the end, we are still within the ordinary. I know perfectly well that by properly guiding and directing the fermentation of my must, it is possible to maximize the generation of natural sulfites, but I am a very small producer and I don't have the means, the money, or the time to achieve this result. And besides, my wine is certainly better than that of any non-organic producer. A bit of sulfur dioxide, potassium bisulfite, or sodium bisulfite, and the fermentation stops to preserve my wine and also those who drink it! If the law allows calling a wine with the characteristics of mine organic, it is precisely to indicate that this wine is the most natural you can find on the market. With my wine, you are safe and have no surprises because it is simply the result of natural operations that humans have been doing for thousands of years.

36 Nuclear waste in the sea [A]

Denise, 9:45 AM on any ordinary day

The issue of energy is very close to my heart. Maybe it's because of the studies I've done on the topic in both academic and personal settings, or perhaps it's a sense of personal responsibility, knowing that we all have a role to play in managing the planet that hosts us. Whatever the reason, I am genuinely interested in energy matters! How do I feel about it? It's simple! It would be wonderful to live in a world where energy is inexhaustible, freely provided to everyone without potential problems caused by nuclear power plants, even those labeled as "zero risk." Unfortunately, this goal, at least for now, remains a chimera, a pure utopia. Radioactive pollution is a serious issue for the planet, and that's why the World Health Organization (WHO) sets strict maximum radioactivity parameters that must be constantly measured, especially around nuclear power plants, to ensure a habitable environment. As I've mentioned before, I'm quite passionate about this topic, and I've read on various reputable web sources that these parameters are very rigorous. The WHO ensures that in samples repeatedly taken from seawater for monitoring purposes, there is not an excessively high concentration of radioactive substances. Specifically, this threshold is set at 10,000 Becquerels per liter of water. I don't want to delve into the tedious explanation of what this unit of measurement represents, but let's just say it signifies radioactivity! Yes, radioactivity in the sea due to water used to cool reactors. Ten thousand, got it? I have no idea how dangerous these 10k Bq are, and I certainly can't adjudicate on that, but if the WHO defines it as a tolerable value, it's certainly well below any harmful threshold. I feel safe!

Nuclear waste in the sea [B]

Denise, 8:30 PM on another ordinary day

Recently, Japan has begun dumping 1.34 million tons of water used to cool the radioactive cores of reactors damaged during the 2011 tsunami into the sea at Fukushima. This is concerning because it involves radioactive water that could eventually enter our bodies or those of animals in this vast marine ecosystem, from which we derive our food, and into fruits and vegetables that are part of our diet. The absurd aspect of this situation is that in Japan, the parameter limit for radioactive contamination of water is much higher than the maximum tolerated by the WHO. In Japan, this threshold is 60,000 Becquerels per liter of water! Although the company managing the plant has assured that the water will be diluted so that radioactivity in samples taken after the discharge is much lower than the WHO limit, I personally find it unjust that a country decides unilaterally to pollute a common resource like the sea. Moreover, this dumping process is expected to last for 30 years. Currently, water samples taken show very low levels of radioactivity, no more than 8 Becquerels per liter. However, global public opinion is convinced that this deliberate act of pollution is not correct and potentially harmful. The international community is also concerned. It is true that other entities, like Dhina, dump into the sea quantities of radioactive water 500 times higher than the limit allowed by the WHO, but there seems to be a double standard in public perception. While I understand that some European disposal centers handle large quantities of radioactive water near residential areas, these centers are considered exemplary and presumed to take all necessary precautions. However, this does not justify further acts of pollution. Who really authorizes further pollution of the sea, which is a common heritage for all?

37 Dream of living in the countryside - I [A]

Giancarlo, 7:00 AM on any given day

I love nature and the peace it brings. I love the countryside, the beauty of landscapes, and the tranquility found there. Yes, I love the countryside, and with it the mountains, rivers, lakes, and sea – places of absolute purity, expressions of unspoiled nature, often far from the chaos of cities, air and noise pollution. These are places of breathtaking beauty where silence is only interrupted by natural sounds – the wind rustling through leaves, birds singing, and little else. No shouts or honking horns, no screeching brakes, no blaring music from nearby stores, no sweaty crowds pushing you around. No stress, no hyperactivity from a thousand commitments, just peace and serenity! Unfortunately, like many, I work in the city and constantly endure stress. It starts from the moment I wake up and lasts all day with extreme multitasking and rapid context switching that drains me. By evening, I'm exhausted, especially psychologically. The sheer amount of information my brain processes during a typical workday is overwhelming. Sure, I try to manage it and I'm good at it, but it's still too much and damaging for anyone. So, I yearn for a break that takes me away from all this, to a place of serenity, to that ancient peace from which we all come, which only unspoiled nature can offer. To unplug, to isolate myself from this frantic world, to retreat into a realm of pure peace and tranquility. A little isolated cottage among trees and the gentle lapping of water is all I want! Give me a quiet spot, a small garden, silence, nature, a bit of food and water – simplicity. That would truly make me happy. And I would love not to come back.

Dream of living in the countryside - I [B]

Giancarlo, 7:00 PM on another ordinary day

My friend surprised me with something incredible! Knowing my desire to spend a few days in the peace of the countryside, he gave me the keys to his house nestled in a forest near the lake! We took time off, and with my wife and kids, we set off for a weekend of relaxation. As soon as we arrived, captivated by the beauty of the place, we settled into outdoor lounge chairs. Now, I wanted to make coffee... I went inside to look for pods, but couldn't find the machine. There was only a moka pot and coffee beans! Oh well... I used the manual grinder. Done! I put the moka pot on the stove. And the gas? Oh, you had to activate the gas cylinder first... Done! Oh no... it's empty! My friend didn't mention that. Maybe he didn't know either. I went down to the valley, bought a new cylinder, came back, and installed it. The coffee tasted strange, but it's almost 8 PM, time for dinner. I'd love to catch up on the day's news, but there's no TV. No problem, I have the dedicated app... What? No connection? Fine, no news. It's probably better this way; disconnecting for a few days will do us good. But on Sunday, there's MotoGP, Formula 1, football... Maybe we'll go down to the valley for lunch. Now, though, I'm going to take a shower... Brrr, the water is cold! Oh right, the water heater is tiny. This countryside house is nice, but it lacks the basics! If it were mine, I'd have ensured all comforts were in place. Otherwise, what kind of vacation is this? Dinner's over, now I need to dispose of the organic waste and... Noooo! No trash bin! I have to carry the rubbish down to the valley myself. I can't believe it! Fortunately, it's time to sleep. I lie down... I'm not used to all this silence. Not that I miss the city noises, but they somehow keep me company at home. Okay, peace and tranquility are nice, but when a countryside house lacks the bare essentials, it gets tough.

38 Hooray for nature, flora, and fauna! [A]

Danila, 7:15 AM on any given day

I love nature in all its forms and expressions. It is our mother after all, and she is a sweet, caring mother... sometimes she becomes severe, but I understand because she defends herself precisely when she wants us to pay for all the abuses we force upon her. But even then, it's not an attack against us, but a defense. Nature is generous, as it allows us to survive thanks to the fruits of the earth, animals, and resources. But nature can also be stingy, when it withholds rains and snows for so long that it jeopardizes the water reserves we strive to create. Nevertheless, we are still her children; she certainly does not forget that. No mother can forget her children. Can we embrace Mother Nature? Of course we can! In fact, I love getting lost in a forest in autumn and smelling its scents, observing its colors. I enjoy walking along freshly beaten paths, in the shade of ancient trees that protect me with their branches. I love all animals, even those most dangerous to humans, who are certainly not to blame for it. Man is nothing but a slightly more evolved animal, certainly the most dangerous, given his intelligence. We must respect nature in all its forms and expressions, for our survival depends on it! We must avoid exterminating entire species, clearing forests to the ground, and bending gentle Mother Nature to our crazy and thoughtless unchecked urbanization. Cities that replace trees, blankets of asphalt that suffocate the soil, towering buildings that take away light, causing the death of birds, cars that kill small mammals. It's a massacre! We are not the center of the universe; we are part of an immensely rich context that also belongs to us but must be protected at all costs. Human supremacism is unsustainable!

Hooray for nature, flora, and fauna! ^B

Danila, 5:00 PM on any other day

This bad smell is unbearable. But what is it? Ah yes... the dung from the cows in the neighboring farm. Ugh, this is unacceptable! I will protest, even if it means joining a group of citizens to have the farm relocated. I don't believe a farmer can let his animals graze without considering the foul odors as a side effect. Come on! I'm not talking about an intensive farm, just a small-scale farmer with his cows. And then there's the farmer storing the manure for months and using it for fertilizer. Seriously? Don't I have the right to breathe clean air? Isn't there anyone monitoring the environmental conditions we live in? We need a municipal office to collect these complaints and act promptly. Right now, there are millions of mosquitoes; I want to exterminate them all. I've asked the administrator to organize pest control in the area. Finally, they'll carry it out tomorrow, and we'll be rid of them for at least a month. Some have suggested I should put up a bat house; apparently, bats devour millions of mosquitoes daily. But please! Should I really keep those very ugly monsters in my house or garden?! They may be useful, but they terrify me, and if there were any around, I would do everything to get rid of them! I have other things to worry about... on the sides of the road leading to our house, invasive weeds are growing. A neighbor - a bit crazy - asks not to remove them because, according to him, they produce beautiful flowers. Maybe so, but it's not normal that I can't park on the roadside and let my passenger out because of these darn weeds. Sure, we should respect nature, flora, and fauna, but there are more pressing needs, or at least what represents the bare minimum for a reasonably peaceful life!

Gamification 4/10

Paragraph	Only A OR B	Both A AND B
23 Dirty streets (in the city)	☐ 0 points	☐ 1 point
24 Dirty streets (outside the city)	☐ 0 points	☐ 1 point
25 Water consumption (at home)	☐ 0 points	☐ 1 point
26 Water consumption (outside the home)	☐ 0 points	☐ 1 point
27 Waste separation	☐ 0 points	☐ 1 point
28 Flora and fauna	☐ 0 points	☐ 1 point
29 Infrastructures	☐ 0 points	☐ 1 point
30 Vehicle maintenance	☐ 0 points	☐ 1 point
31 Electric vehicles	☐ 0 points	☐ 1 point
32 Ecology and coherence	☐ 0 points	☐ 1 point
33 Ecology and protest	☐ 0 points	☐ 1 point
34 Ecology and habits	☐ 0 points	☐ 1 point
35 Organic food and beverages	☐ 0 points	☐ 1 point
36 Nuclear waste in the sea	☐ 0 points	☐ 1 point
37 Dream of living in the countryside - I	☐ 0 points	☐ 1 point
38 Hooray for nature, flora and fauna	☐ 0 points	☐ 1 point
TOTAL		

World of work

Sometimes I spend the entire meeting wondering how they managed to get the big table through the door.

Anonymous

39 Career and networking [A]

Aloisio, 10:30 AM on any given day

I entered the company, so to speak, through the 'back door'. I saw the job posting on a portal and applied. In the interview, I was selected for a role different from what I had hoped for, but... work is work! Over the years, I have taken many steps forward. Now, I lead a team of colleagues and am respected and valued! My coworkers love me because I don't just give orders; I get my hands dirty alongside them. I'm the first to start and the last to finish. It's not authoritarianism from me; it's authority! When we complete a project, the credit goes to everyone, not just me. But if something goes wrong, I willingly step in between my colleagues and my superiors to protect them. A reprimand from the boss could be so demoralizing for them. For me, however, all the boss's reprimands just roll off me like warm water. I treat my colleagues almost like my children and feel a deep empathy with them. When they ask for vacation days or a few hours off, I approve it without hesitation. Anyone who thinks personal needs should be subordinate to the company's is completely wrong. Employees and companies sign a contract that holds legal value. National contracts are written to protect this relationship from both sides and establish a set number of hours that must be compensated with equivalent, or nearly equivalent, money. Are there companies that give away money for no reason? No! Similarly, no employee should give away hours to the company without fair compensation on their paycheck. This is the basic rule for me, and my team colleagues know it. Do you think I'm foolish? I might lose a few euros in production bonuses, but the team harmony that this approach fosters is priceless.

Career and networking [B]

Aloisio, 6:30 PM on another random day

I've been promoted within the company and now I'm among 'those who matter'. We're talking about the team of managers, just below the top boss! Honestly, I never thought I could be so happy about this, but being invited to all the strategic meetings makes me feel good. And, this change has also had some small economic benefits, which doesn't hurt. Perhaps the greatest satisfaction, though, is looking back at the journey I've taken to get here. Of course, I've had to change my habits and relationships with colleagues. My old teammates now have a different manager, and naturally, our relationship isn't the same as it was when we worked side by side on projects. I'm no longer their direct supervisor, it's true, but I'm hierarchically above their new boss. I couldn't intervene even if I wanted to, as I used to! Sometimes I hear their bosses speak badly of them, but I no longer step in to defend them. I have a new role now, and one can't always be oppositional towards superiors. They lead a tough life to keep things running and need people nearby who support them, not those who oppose them at every turn. Now that I'm on the other side, I understand how lonely it can feel to lead something big, and how crucial those few collaborators are who have the privilege of being close to the ultimate leader. Unfortunately, sometimes I'm asked to report on less-than-praiseworthy behaviors exhibited by employees, and I have to do so. But it's for the good of the company, so I absolve myself easily. After all, we all pursue a greater good that necessarily transcends individual interests.

40 Colleagues and confidences [A]

Ignazio, 8:15 AM on any given day

I have a best friend at work to whom I tell everything, confide everything. His name is Sempronio. We're inseparable! You know, each of us can boast of having a best friend, even at work. One of those you can easily tell who might be the next to resign! One you can share your bonus figures with without triggering envy, talk about your raise without fearing they'll say anything to anyone! Then I have a friend who's a bit less present but equally loyal... his name is Tizio. I can tell him everything, absolutely everything! I don't even need to ask him to keep things confidential, he does it naturally, he's a vault, I can absolutely trust his loyalty! I just told him something that happened to my dear friend Sempronio, something he didn't want me to tell anyone! But I can definitely tell my friend Tizio because he's a vault... Then, of course, besides the best friend with a capital 'B', there's another dear friend, Lucy, to whom I tell fewer things, not the too-secret ones, but still somewhat... classified. My friend Lucy is sweet and beautiful, how can you keep secrets from her? I ask her not to tell anyone because I trust her a bit less, but she's still a friend and deep down I know she would never betray me. I told her about Sempronio, she was surprised and assured me she wouldn't tell anyone. Finally, I have one last friend to whom I tell even less important things, but sometimes, in an excess of confidence, I tell him everything anyway because we've known each other for years and I know I can trust him in some way too. When I ask him to keep a secret, he understands perfectly how to handle the information I'm giving him. It was the same with Sempronio... But come to think of it, there are a few more friends after all...

Colleagues and confidences [B]

Ignazio, 4:30 PM on another random day

The word has spread! All my colleagues found out that Dinetto got the raise while others who have been asking for it for a long time didn't! And there's another problem... Pistoio is angry with me... he claims that I told others things he had confided to me in a private conversation, things he asked me to keep secret, and I had sworn! He basically accuses me of spreading rumors about his affair with colleague Cunegonda. But what does that have to do with me? Absurd! He must have talked about it with who knows how many other "friends" of his; he can't keep a secret to save his life. And besides, I had told Sempronio about the affair and Tizio about the raise, but they would never put me in trouble like this. I ask Pistoio where this accusation comes from, and he says Triscillo heard it from Petrosia, who was told by Rigino, who Marielletta spilled the beans to, claiming she heard it from... Sempronio! Damn it! I trusted him. What a betrayal!! I ask him to keep a secret, and this is how he repays me? But seriously... if I'm telling you something sensitive that nobody knows and shouldn't be spread around, especially about colleagues, how can you then blabber about it to anyone? How could he betray our eternal pact of confidentiality like this? Truly absurd. I'm deeply disappointed, and I don't know if I can forgive such a betrayal. He's a rat, a snitch! And anyway, going back to Pistoio's outburst, who knows how many people he's told this to, not just me. In fact, knowing that I'm a vault when it comes to these things, it's much more likely the loose lips are elsewhere. So, go ahead and vent, dear Pis, but don't forget who you can truly trust!

41 In praise of meritocracy [A]

Erica, 2:45 PM on any given day

There aren't many rules to follow to advance in one's career within the company. For me, there's practically only one: meritocracy. I am a staunch believer in meritocracy. There's not much more to explain. The capable ones should move forward, period. Those who are less driven, who probably don't even want to take honorable steps forward, should stay in their place. I'm not saying to stand idly by, but it simply doesn't make sense to elevate them in the hierarchy because... they just don't deserve it! And if they don't even desire it, then it makes absolutely no sense at all. I have always worked hard and well, excelling in my job. I've never missed a beat, and above all, I have a strong sense of responsibility towards my activities in the company. If there's someone more capable, I would give them space without a second thought, of course! I would even mentor them... curious and eager to learn new things and acquire new skills that can propel me to a higher professional level! Meritocracy comes first and foremost, driven by that natural impulse towards improvement that has always propelled me. If someone deserves it, they should move forward; if they deserve less or don't deserve it at all, they should move backward or stay where they have chosen to stay. There's no room for favoritism. I detest that term; it's as base, archaic, stifling, and above all, unjust as it can be. There's no doubt about it, favoritism is something from the past century, or even before. And it makes no sense. Claiming that someone who's been there for 20 years deserves perks without doing anything exceptional is simply unacceptable. If you've been there for 20 years and haven't done anything different from what you did on the first day, then you deserve less than the newest arrival!

In praise of meritocracy ^B

Erica, 4:15 PM on another random day

A new colleague has recently arrived in the office, a very young one. I think his name is Pretellio. He was hired to support me because I couldn't handle all the tasks alone anymore. He's sharp, I could tell from the first moment, and he's very kind to everyone. And, not to mention, he's very good at the tasks he was hired for, I must admit. But I am who I am, and he is who he is, let's not kid ourselves. Yesterday in a meeting, they assigned tasks to Pretellio that used to be under my responsibility, and that bothered me. I have to be honest, until he arrived, I couldn't manage all of it alone anymore, but maybe now, with the support he's brought in other areas, I could. But that's not the point. The company is pleased with him, and my boss always compliments him. He says he's very good, but in my opinion, it's just the effect of his younger age, which gives him an image of energy and freshness. However, something terrible happened today. The boss called us in and practically gave him... my role! It's absurd! He may bring new knowledge, but what about the experience I've accumulated in nearly 30 years here?! How can they take away this role from me and give it to a newcomer? Ok, they are moving me to another department, which will bring new challenges, and they are doing it precisely because my experience could be valuable elsewhere, but what about my ability to manage countless processes? Will they be in his hands now? It's not fair, things shouldn't be done like this, you can't erase so many years with a stroke of a brush. Seniority surely has value! I'm not talking about crude favoritism, about those who expect wonders without giving anything in return, but about an employee, myself, who has contributed immensely to the company's evolution. Where would this company be today without my contributions over all these years?

42 In praise of professionalism [A]

Isidoro, 2:30 PM on any given day

In my company, we are always looking for new professionals of great value and competence. Here, experience and professionalism are genuinely respected! Each colleague has well-defined tasks and applies their knowledge to them without getting involved in a thousand other tasks, and especially without encroaching on others' fields. This is not so much due to jealousy over roles, but rather because it's right that those who have studied and worked hard to perform a particular role, for which they were selected by us, should be able to work in that area without constantly being interrupted by tasks outside their job description that would waste their time. Time is precious and expensive, and it should be used for high-level, equally rewarding tasks! I reiterate, our company greatly values professionalism, and each person is treated according to their own strengths and expertise. We always strive to place the best individuals on projects that suit them best, so they can perform to the best of their abilities, based on their studies and career choices. When someone needs support, a new colleague to help them complete their tasks on time, perhaps because the business is growing, we conduct a careful selection process that involves those who have requested the assistance. We review candidates' resumes, conduct several interviews, with the most crucial one being with the head of the relevant department. Only if we find the right person do we proceed with mutual acquaintance during a probationary period, which typically, if all goes well, transitions into a permanent contract! Professionalism is a core value for us!

In praise of professionalism [B]

Isidoro, 8:30 AM on another random day

Few years ago, we launched a new product on the market, the Flesione, which has been performing exceptionally well ever since, steadily increasing in terms of revenue. To boost our balance sheet, we had to limit the number of workers assigned to the production lines. Now, however, the success of the Flesione requires new personnel, and the production line manager, Fridrigo, can no longer handle everything alone! He requested to be supported by someone with experience. We identified several candidates and conducted interviews with them, involving Fridrigo who has the final say as our most competent employee in Flesione production. He appreciated several profiles, but one in particular he promoted enthusiastically, recognizing uncommon skills. We tried to secure this candidate, but encountered several challenges. Firstly, the candidate was accustomed to remote work, and we immediately informed him that this is not possible in our company. He asked for explanations, and we simply stated that it's not feasible, period. Another issue was the salary expectations, which were significantly higher than our norms. At that point, Fridrigo requested to consider someone less experienced but possessing basic assembly line production skills, to avoid starting from scratch, which would triple the training time and worsen the situation. We searched for such a candidate but couldn't find anyone at a sufficiently low cost. Therefore, we decided to hire Tometto, an 18-year-old who has just finished school. Yes, he lacks competence, but he costs us nothing, and Fridrigo will have to accept it!

43 In praise of planning [A]

Eva, 12:35 on any given day

There are various processes that keep a company running, but some of them are only truly understood and appreciated when the number of projects grows, along with the team working on them. One of the most important processes is planning. Managing work timelines, allocating resources, prioritizing tasks – these are essential in any project activity. You simply cannot effectively manage something as complex as a project without breaking it down into smaller parts and carefully scheduling them! Planning is crucial from the first to the last day of scheduled activities. How else could you manage deadlines, deliveries, make forecasts, calculate budgets, decide on staffing needs, measure KPIs, etc.? We create a plan every time a new project starts and then, during its execution, we strive to adhere to it, updating or modifying it only in extreme cases to ensure everything runs smoothly and as expected. Of course, in the event of a genuine emergency – something so serious that it necessitates reallocating resources and consequently postponing previously planned activities – then adjustments must be made accordingly. After all, planning is one of the cornerstones of project management. Such contingencies are also addressed in the best practice guidelines governing its rules. It's clear that we're talking about a real emergency here, something that absolutely cannot be left to chance, hoping it will resolve itself. It's something that requires the attention of the entire company. Routine events of minor importance should not disrupt the overall planning.

In praise of planning [B]

Eva, 4:35 PM on another random day

A problem has just occurred on the production line of our product Liquid Xaprino. The customer, Liquiditudini Inc., contacted us directly with their CEO Markucc Smith, requesting to speak with our own CEO Svetlano Abitudi. In a fit of uncontrollable anger, Mr. Abitudi berated us over the issue. It appears that the back label, visible through the transparency when Xaprino is finished or nearing completion, displays the contact email in small bold font instead of regular font, smaller even than Uncle Scrooge's fine print. While this might seem a minor issue for less critical customers, it has become an absolute catastrophe for a primary client like Liquiditudini – the kind of issue the English would describe as "mind-blowing" and could seriously damage the reputation of the manufacturing company and us, who always pride ourselves on meticulous attention to detail. Our reputation holds immense value, perhaps the most precious to us. Therefore, we now face a company-wide emergency, necessitating immediate revision of our plans to address it. Whenever serious emergencies like this arise, our plans must be adjusted to meet them head-on. It is clear why the principle of "ubi maior minor cessat" applies here. Project managers argue that reallocating resources from ongoing projects, even temporarily, will jeopardize meeting deadlines and exacerbate problems manifold, but we cannot entertain such arguments. An emergency is an emergency and must be treated as such. Moreover, this client brings in substantial revenue upon which all our salaries depend. Therefore, everyone needs to be fully engaged and proactive in resolving this issue!

44 Overwork ^A

Manlia, 11:30 AM on any given day

I dislike those who waste time at work, those who always seem stressed by activities... fake! You find them around at any moment, sometimes they go out to smoke and stay there for half an hour, then you find them in front of the coffee machine for another half hour, then in the bathroom again for half an hour, and then chatting with colleagues. They always complain to others about the unbearable weight of their work activities. It's safe to say, without exaggerating too much, that these are people who leech off the company for at least three or four hours every day. But does this seem tolerable to you? All of this magnifies the annoyance and suffering of colleagues who do not behave like this. Those who actually work are significantly harmed by this behavior. They often perceive salaries equal to or lower than those of these time-wasters, yet they work much harder, my goodness do they work hard, and feel a strong sense of injustice because of it. Ironically, precisely because they work so hard, the few times they take a break, there are even those who criticize them for it. For example, I work a lot, I'm always involved in the tasks assigned to me, and I take very few, really very few breaks during the workday. I perceive this difference very clearly, but I can't do anything about it. It's not that I don't want my colleagues to take breaks or enjoy themselves occasionally at work, but what bothers me is the amount of time spent on total leisure rather than work. Unfortunately, those who should be aware of this know nothing about it. Either upper management becomes aware of these behaviors and finds a way to limit them, or the frustration of people like me will skyrocket and it won't be good for anyone. No doctor prescribed me to work here!

Overwork [B]

Manlia, 1:00 PM on another random day

I find it unacceptable that my colleagues who preceded me on this project did such a poor job that I've inherited such a terrible situation. I will try to fix it, but unspeakable mistakes were made. I can't pretend otherwise. I look for my colleague Pinino, greet him, and tell him what I found when taking over the project, emphasizing how absurdly low the quality level of those who worked before me is. Then I go to my colleagues Manuccio, Marchello, and Guidonio and tell them the same thing. I appreciate their sympathetic looks towards the old guard of the project, because that look acknowledges my great abilities, skills, and professionalism, which are well-known throughout the company. They all know here how good I am. I sit back down and discover an email from a subordinate colleague, Henrietto. It almost seems like he wants to give me orders. I am truly outraged, how dare he? Does he realize he's talking to someone who truly understands? One of those who has truly driven the company forward for so long, working as if there's no tomorrow, and whose work is truly invaluable? I can't keep this to myself, I must discuss it with my colleagues at the same level, Gregonio and Artusio. I forward them the email and quickly join them, with a smile that they immediately interpret as I see them. And they begin to nod their heads as if to say... poor guy, forgive him, he doesn't know what he's doing. I express all my anger towards Henrietto to them and tell them I will respond in kind. Oh, he'll hear from me! Me, who handles such an immense workload every day that no one else could manage! No, that's not enough, I have to tell Gignetta and Frubonio about this! Here, I write the response. I edit it for two hours and then return to my colleagues to discuss it...

45 Workplace fatalities [A]

Leandro, 11:45 AM on any given day

The news anchor has just read today's news and once again announced the workplace deaths of three people. It's absurd that in this day and age, events like these still occur. It's absurd that a person loses their life while working to earn money to support themselves and their family in a dignified manner. The state must do something; this is no longer about isolated, infrequent incidents. We are talking about hundreds and hundreds of people losing their lives every year at their workplaces! I am a handyman in a construction company and, as such, I am particularly affected by this issue, given the numerous fields in which I work. Next Saturday, we will take to the streets to protest against this massacre. Urgent measures are needed, effective laws, and companies that respect the safety of their employees. Workplace safety is certainly a very serious issue in all countries of the world, but here it seems to be particularly severe. Workers falling from scaffolding at construction sites, others being hit by objects falling from above, others dying inside boilers they are cleaning or being crushed in extremely dangerous machinery. Companies claim to be compliant and declare themselves not guilty, but it is evident that this cannot be the case. It is clear that they are responsible for the frequent violations of basic safety rules. The employees, the workers, those who ultimately do the dirty work firsthand, are an invaluable asset to the company. How is it possible to let them work in dangerous conditions? How is it possible that a father never returns home after a day's work? That a son, on his first experience in a company, dies in such a horrific way? This must never happen again!

Workplace fatalities [B]

Leandro, 7:35 AM on another ordinary day

Today I started my work at the construction site at 7:00 AM, going up and down the scaffolding hundreds of times between the 12 floors of the building. I'm with a very young and inexperienced colleague. I'm trying to train him, but he's incredibly slow. Imagine that with every move, he puts on and takes off his safety harness. Sure, I should be wearing them too, but for me, they are unnecessary... do you realize the value of my twenty years of experience on these scaffolds? I'm meeting all the scheduled deadlines for my work, and besides, I like feeling free which allows me to move quickly. Not that I wouldn't ever wear them, I know they are a mandatory safety measure, but do you know how much time it takes to attach and detach the harness from one floor to the next each time? Do you have any idea how limited your movements are when wearing it and how slowly it forces you to work? Okay, safety is important, but what could possibly happen to me? I'm very experienced and I know every single risk of my job. Accidents happen to rookies, not to experienced people like me. The same goes for painting; I breathe terribly with the mask on. I don't need it! I know how to control my breathing, use my nose, and turn away when there are particularly dense fumes. When we clean the tanks, I know exactly when one has been open long enough to be safe. Surely, those who died inside didn't have my experience. The company has always provided everything needed to protect me. Masks, harnesses, training, refresher courses, signs everywhere to remind us to use all these protective devices. But it's clear that the company also relies on my extensive experience, and I trust my own judgment regarding danger completely.

46 Projects and manuals [A]

Fabiola, 2:35 PM on any given day

Every project, regardless of its type, must be accompanied by manuals, instructions for use, analysis documents, and in short, textual comments of any kind that allow those who will analyze the completed work later to understand every detail of the choices made, the functioning of the systems, and every aspect almost as if they were inside the mind of the person who implemented the project. Every day, I face issues arising from a lack of manuals and documentation due to engineers and designers who are too hasty to finish the product development, aiming to bring it to market, for sale, or into operation as quickly as possible, depending on the type of project. And it's painful! So much superficiality and lack of professionalism! It's terrible to have to understand, in the absence of documentation, what was going through the mind of the person who designed that solution. Damn it! It's not easy at all to interpret someone else's thoughts after the fact. It's already difficult to revisit your own designs at a later time, let alone things designed by someone else, different from you, distant in time, methods, and experiences. And the risk of making a mistake during maintenance is very high. It's like constructing a building without a blueprint, a map, or a drawing. If one day I wanted to reinforce the pillars, how could I ever know where they are, as they are completely hidden, covered, and painted over? The only possible way to find them would be to drill everywhere to check what's behind the plaster. In short, documentation should be mandatory for every project in the world and, above all, qualitatively valid because it is ethically wrong to think that a project ends when the artifact is completed.

Projects and manuals [B]

Fabiola, 11:30 AM on another ordinary day

Today, my boss called me, asking me to momentarily leave my daily activities to dedicate myself to a special project. Our company is participating in a bid for a very important contract with an even more significant prospective client. Our future depends on this, and I'm in line for a promotion. Yes, because time is short and my boss, knowing my great problem-solving skills and speed in implementing solutions, has placed me at the center of a group of equally capable people. Unfortunately, we decided to enter this bid only a few days ago. We will need to be quick, disregard the unnecessary, and focus on the project to arrive at a functioning simulation as soon as possible. We must instinctively recognize the activities that waste time, can be postponed, or do not add value to the finished product. We will write the project by concentrating all our efforts on the primary goal: reaching the day of the simulation with something that works. Documentation, comments, descriptions, instructions? This is not the time to dedicate ourselves to that stuff, which is important, yes, but does not contribute to the actual functioning of the product. The day when someone has to modify what we've done? Let's first worry about making it work, making it impressive and effective, and winning the bid, then we'll concern ourselves with those things that come only after these stages. We're talking about serious stuff here, a historic opportunity, and we can't waste time! Besides, I am very clear when I write projects; I challenge anyone to tackle them… they would understand them even if they were a child. Documentation isn't even necessary, believe me. If the boss chose me, it's because I'm the best.

47 Yes-men and women [A]

Ivano, 12:00 PM on any given day

Everyone knows what one of the most serious diseases of any company is: *yes-women* and *yes-men*. It doesn't mean they aren't good people in their personal lives, of course, but when it comes to their involvement in high-level management of companies, I have a lot to criticize. *Yes-persons* are a real cancer that eats away at the company from within and constantly worsens its performance. We're talking about people who work closely with the company's leadership and participate in all decision-making meetings. They have the power, at least theoretically, to voice their own opinion and, if it differs from that of the boss, to challenge it and propose different actions. I am not a *yes-man*. I have never been one and never could be. If someone calls me into a meeting, it's because they are interested in hearing my seasoned opinion on an issue and want to listen to how I would resolve it. It's this honesty of mine that makes me invaluable in times when effective action is needed. I'm not afraid of the impact my words might have on the boss; in fact, I couldn't care less. If he asks for my opinion, it's because he's interested in knowing it, regardless of how different it may be from his own thinking. Ultimately, he can do as he pleases; after all, he's the boss! But I will never be a *yes-man* never. Moreover, when I assert certain things, I do so because I firmly believe in them, not out of a foolish and dangerous spirit of opposition. If the boss says something foolish, I must point it out. If he decides to treat someone unfairly, I must suggest a more analytical and less brutal course of action. That's my role, that's what I'm paid to do: serve the company's best interests, not to blindly agree with opinions I don't believe in at all.

Yes-men and women [B]

Ivano, 4:30 PM on another ordinary day

Today the boss is really angry. Something happened that he considers serious, and he is furious. As always when this happens, he is making a series of overly drastic decisions, without considering the time needed to implement them and, above all, the actual effectiveness of the consequent actions! When moments like these occur, one should not act impulsively, but rather gather together, put all the possibilities on the table, and calmly decide which to implement, which to cancel, and which to postpone. I have my own opinion on what happened, but I'm careful not to voice it today. Or rather, I tried, but as soon as I understood the mood he is in, I gave up. I don't want to risk my career. It might not seem too strange, but when we are in these phases, I certainly don't point out all the negative implications that these impulsive actions generate. I stay close by and somehow go along with what he is deciding. Okay, we live in a free country, I have acquired the right to speak from the constitution, the national contract, and the company regulations, but I don't want to ruin my career just to state my opinion. The boss is at a stage in his professional journey where he terribly detests any contrary opinion. Paradoxically, a colleague friend accuses me of behaving like a *yes-man*... what? Me, a *yes-man*? Are you kidding? I'm not living the emperor's new clothes syndrome, where the supreme boss says wrong things, talks about unachievable goals, defines estimates he cannot define due to incompetence, and everyone present to these actions nods, consents, accepts, approves. I'm just offering support, in a difficult moment, to him who has infinitely more responsibilities than I do!

48 The boss's responsibilities [A]

Dorotea, 10:00 AM on any given day

I have been running this company for many years, relying on my personal and professional skills. These abilities are absolutely fundamental for an entrepreneur like me and have been developed over the years thanks to the experience I've accumulated. But if my talent had not been at the foundation of all this, and especially my innate ability to generate profit from ideas, things, people, by inventing new products and services, probably no one in my company would be here today. I have achieved something truly great! We have grown tremendously and are now known and renowned everywhere. We are esteemed, invited to every forum... At every presentation, we are there! Let it be clear... I did not achieve all this alone; my skill was also in surrounding myself with the right people from the beginning and continuing to do so even today. Certainly, my self-esteem makes me confidently affirm that I was the driving force behind everything, but then necessarily I had to seek talent in others, those who would have to work in areas where I could no longer be involved. Delegating was difficult, I admit. When a company is small and there are few of us, everyone does everything, so each team member is responsible for a very long series of activities and processes. Then, gradually, as the company grows, you have to slowly hand over your responsibilities to others who will have that particular task as their sole (or almost sole) task and will perform it to the best of their abilities, or at least that is the hope. And I, as a woman leading this company, have had to delegate countless activities to others. Of course, I chose competent people whom I trust completely; otherwise, I wouldn't have made it! It's difficult when it happens, but it is the only way to truly make everything grow.

The boss's responsibilities [B]

Dorotea, 4:15 PM on another given day

I walk through the corridors of my company almost every day. I enjoy watching my colleagues diligently working on their tasks. I still handle many responsibilities, but they are finally more suited to my role. I admit that I don't mind being faced with ordinary problems. When I see confusion on the faces of participants in a meeting, I step in without hesitation. No one can turn me away, right? Being the boss has its perks! When it comes to discussing new features to add to somewhat stale products, I generate a series of ideas that the others present could never come up with. Then I order them to add these features to this or that product. Other times we discuss processes. Here, too, I bring out innovative proposals that leave everyone stunned. They all look at me with their mouths agape. Sometimes they raise objections, which I immediately dismantle. They rarely oppose, but it does happen. For example, today we were discussing new features to add to a service, and the project manager and the marketing manager had conducted surveys, obtaining results based on which they had decided on the necessary features. I gave my opinion, stating that the most important feature was another one. They started insisting because the data suggested otherwise, but you know what? I don't care! I have talent and have become so accustomed to it that I trust its signals blindly. Some say that excessive confidence in one's talent can become an excuse not to think and not to seek support. But if the idea comes to me, there is always a kernel of truth in it. I am certain that this feature will be successful. I silenced the colleague by telling him to do as I asked, period. Then I left. Discussing the obvious bores me. Some employees are so devoid of talent...

49 Overtime [A]

Fiorenza, 8:00 AM on any given day

I love working! The job I am fortunate to do is exactly what I dreamed of: producing everyday objects. If you do your duty and achieve the daily quota of products on our assembly line, you can really be at ease. Many young people, knowing I am a veteran, ask me about various things, including overtime. Well, it's simple! The employment contract between the company and the employee is governed by law and involves a fair exchange between the employee's work performance and the company's money. The latter is meant to compensate fairly (or almost) for the work performed. An employee must work the number of hours stipulated in the contract and be paid accordingly. If they work more, the company must pay more, of course. My company does not allow unpaid overtime. To work extra hours, you need to get permission from your supervisor. All this makes sense; otherwise, anyone could stay here several extra hours every day without necessity and earn unjustly, thus taking more money. Paid overtime is when every extra hour worked corresponds to extra money in the paycheck. Requiring unpaid overtime is obviously illegal, and no honest company in the world would ever ask for it. But even giving away hours of your own will to the company is completely wrong! Have you ever found extra money in your paycheck under the label "gift"? Would it seem credible if the company decided to freely gift employees €100 at the end of the month? No! So why should an employee give away hours of their private life, thereby distorting the company's productive capacity to the extent that it can no longer provide reliable estimates of planned activities?

Overtime [B]

Fiorenza, 5:00 PM on another given day

My work unit is under stress right now. Our flagship product breaks under certain stresses, and ironically, it seems the cause is traced to the paint used during the coloring process, a choice that came from my office, hence from me as the responsible person. How can this be? It appears that a specific substance in the enamel we chose damages the plastic material fibers deeply, leading to the fragility of the entire piece. I need everyone's help! We need to focus on this problem. There are several fronts to work on... The first is to verify if there was indeed a declared specific incompatibility between the two. If there wasn't, so be it, it's not our fault. If there was, we'll have to take responsibility towards the company, and tough days will follow. The second is to find a solution for the products already on sale. The third is to choose different paints for the products we'll make from now on. It's the end of the workday, and I see the first colleagues leaving for home. I stop them! I ask why they're leaving, and they respond that I always emphasized the importance of respecting work hours. They assumed this rule applied universally. But no! That's not the case. There's a tangible, serious emergency that directly concerns them, and they're leaving? They say if it had been considered overtime, they would have stayed. Overtime? You've created the problem, and now the company should pay you to fix it? Are we crazy? Fine, go ahead, but we will definitely take this into account in the year-end evaluations. It's absurd not to be willing to work more in emergency situations.

50 No more smart working [A]

Iacopo, 8:00 AM on any given day

For various reasons, I don't believe in smart working. Employees need to be supervised, otherwise they either don't work or work much less than they could. Moreover, I believe that the personal connection that forms when people physically meet in the office builds the team, strengthens personal and professional relationships, and makes everyone more determined to achieve common goals. I had to allow smart working during a recent epidemic only because otherwise I would have had to shut down all operations at my plastic laminate factory for two years! That would probably have been the end of us. I can't deny that our productivity during that period didn't decrease; our engineers continued to work diligently, perhaps because when you're working smart, you can't be anywhere else but in front of your screen. However, I still believe that face-to-face interaction is crucial. I think even my own designers experienced this, although they would never admit it! Smart working can't work because if employees aren't monitored, they're inclined to waste time. And I'm not just talking about working less; I mean when they wander around the house in slippers, making coffee after coffee, playing with their kids, or going grocery shopping or washing their car! Yes, I know the law mandates a break every 2 hours, but in smart working, everything can be a break! Essentially, if someone wanted to, they could never work, always be on vacation. But then, do you really think that staring at a sterile screen allows you to feel the vibes of a meeting room? To perceive the true passion, doubts, hopes of colleagues when discussing this or that project? To create a real bond within a team? No, smart working won't happen in my company anymore. Unless there are new pandemics, it's just a sad past memory.

No more smart working [B]

Iacopo, 11:00 AM on another given day

When we gather in the meeting room, often there are many of us and the space is tight. Our headquarters is very small and lacks other gathering areas. At this point, I question the sense of wasting time moving around! In in-person meetings, there's always someone arriving late, someone suggesting coffee before we start, someone talking about their favorite sports team, car races... the weather! Are we really sure that meeting in person is advantageous? We're cramped in the office now, I've rearranged employees several times, but the problem recurs periodically. I still believe that only by working in person can we experience the emotions of relationships and truly be effective on projects. However, it's equally true that wasting time means losing money. So, what's wrong with having remote meetings while sitting at our desks in our offices? This way, we preserve human relationships and shorten the time. To improve performance, we send each other a link and have a video call from our offices. No, it's not like being there in person, obviously; nothing beats human contact. Also, this way I can better monitor employees who certainly won't wander around in their underwear. There are other situations that require this... for example, when an employee working on an important project suddenly goes on long-term sick leave. If a colleague, fearing falling behind, proposes to work from home, I certainly can't accept it because it's against the law. But if they independently decide to lend a hand, why should I stop them? If there were an inspection, it would be their problem. I certainly didn't authorize them to do that!

51 Innovative entrepreneurs [A]

Giulio, 8:00 AM on any given day

I am a successful entrepreneur, one of those who made it and turned an idea, the prefabricated shower, that initially seemed absurd and out of context into a modern technological asset. Essential in this case, and in all similar cases to mine, was timing. Being a first mover provides an unmatched competitive advantage, at least for a certain period. Sure, maybe after years competitors catch up, achieve similar results, uncover your secrets, and imitate you, narrowing that advantage. However, if you stay the course, you'll always remain ahead, even if slightly. How did I get here? Well, it's easier said than done: continuous updating! It's my mantra, my absolute rule. I've always been fascinated by innovations, by new things promising to make life easier. While others feared them because they disrupted the tranquility of ordinary and cyclical ways of doing things, I was the first to try, to experiment. From these experiments came new ideas, new insights for further progress. And my products have always been at the forefront. Yes, because if you're always in favor of changing, modifying, improving for the benefit of the end customer, the customer rewards you with loyalty! My product is still pure innovation; every new technology released, I examine it, verify it, integrate it, learn lessons about what to do and what not to do, and then implement it by asking my employees to become experts, absolute masters of it. I don't care about the company cost this imposes on my production line because it's the only way to remain absolutely competitive in this market. At this point, I can confidently and proudly say that it's the only valid way to work today.

Innovative entrepreneurs [B]

Giulio, 4:30 PM on another typical day

Recently, we seized a great opportunity: acquiring the project of a not-so-new competitor product, the "bathtub for wheelchairs", which holds an exclusive market share. We purchased the project from an entrepreneur transitioning to consultancy. He and I are profoundly different, but I understand his decision! The life of a CEO is too stressful to sustain indefinitely. But let's get back to our purchase... there are customers specifically interested in the bathtub's features. I'll meet the first one shortly, and he seems eager and willing to pay well to include it in his catalog. The bathtub I acquired is old and has several flaws that could be addressed today, but this would come at a significant cost. I knew this well when I decided to proceed, but it's precisely because of these issues that I negotiated the price down and made a good deal! In our company, we wanted to acquire a product like this because it complements our offerings. However, thinking about it, our customer doesn't seem to have high expectations... I'm almost tempted to sell him our new acquisition as is, without fixing its issues. What's the point of wasting even a single day of work to replace that part with another similar one just because it's the current trend? Not all new technologies need to be learned and implemented. If something works, why change it? Often, innovation is a trend, something to boast about, but it must make sense; otherwise, it's just wasted time and money. With all due respect, if my customer is satisfied as it is, why invest additional effort? Furthermore, even if I were to modify the components and the underlying technology, the product would still look the same from the outside! So why waste resources if there's no visible difference?

Gamification 5/10

Paragraph	Only A OR B	Both A AND B
39 Career and networking	☐ 0 points	☐ 1 point
40 Colleagues and confidences	☐ 0 points	☐ 1 point
41 In praise of meritocracy	☐ 0 points	☐ 1 point
42 I praise of professionalism	☐ 0 points	☐ 1 point
43 In praise of planning	☐ 0 points	☐ 1 point
44 Overwork	☐ 0 points	☐ 1 point
45 Workplace fatalities	☐ 0 points	☐ 1 point
46 Projects and manuals	☐ 0 points	☐ 1 point
47 Yes-men and women	☐ 0 points	☐ 1 point
48 The boss's responsibilities	☐ 0 points	☐ 1 point
49 Overtime	☐ 0 points	☐ 1 point
50 No more smart working	☐ 0 points	☐ 1 point
51 Innovative entrepreneurs	☐ 0 points	☐ 1 point
TOTAL		

State, politics, services

In men, there truly exists only one consistency: that of their contra-dictions.

Guido Morselli

52 The National Health Service [A]

Artemisia, 11:38 on any given day

The public healthcare system in my country is a complete mess. Appointments are scheduled far into the future, there's rampant absenteeism, lack of attention to detail, and a pervasive culture of shifting responsibility! Today, I urgently requested an appointment, truly urgent, not an exaggeration, and they've scheduled it for at least 2 years from now, by which time my condition will likely be critical or I could even be dead! I needed some routine blood tests, and the proposed date is a staggering 6 months away! What are the causes of all this? Firstly, the ability of doctors to see private patients using public facilities creates an obvious conflict of interest that even a newborn could understand. But beyond this, the real issue is... connections! Many people don't respect their place in line or on the waiting list but instead exert pressure on relatives, acquaintances, or friends of friends to secure a faster appointment. This behavior is disgraceful, uncivil, and disrupts the scheduling of appointments within the National Health Service. Those who follow the rules and have no influential connections are left languishing with no hope of moving up unless they, too, resort to networking. These unfortunate individuals are bypassed by those seeking preferential treatment for their supposedly more urgent needs, which they believe are more important than anyone else's. To make matters worse, every one of these people claims that the National Health Service doesn't work properly! Clearly, they preach one thing and practice another! If every time they need specialist care they resort to underhand methods to jump the queue, how can the service ever function properly?

The National Health Service [B]

Artemisia, 12:45 on another random day

My daughter is not well and urgently needs thorough examinations. She is very young, in the prime of her life, and as a mother, I am terribly afraid for her health. Anything that raises doubts about her real state of health is an alert that I absolutely cannot ignore. And now there's this strangeness, this sudden discomfort, these worrying signs that I will certainly not let pass without the utmost concern. I cannot afford expensive private specialist visits that would undoubtedly provide reliable results with lightning speed. However, I still need to quickly find a way to get her seen by a good specialist, a renowned expert, in short. Thinking about it... I have a friend, Morrio, who works in the field and owes me quite a few favors. He boasts of being close to someone who matters, really matters, at least around here. Well, I can't dwell on it too much. This is a serious urgency. We're not talking about a toothache or an ingrown toenail, but something worrying. I don't want to ignore these signs and regret it later! I called my friend and explained the situation to him. He was reassuring and said he would quickly take care of it. And so he contacted the big shot, explaining the situation thoroughly. Well, my friend is truly close to this luminary, because within a few hours, I received a call from the hospital to schedule the appointment... for tomorrow! It may seem unethical and unfair, but can you compare it to the health of a daughter? Maybe I wouldn't do it for someone else, but for her, I would do anything. And besides, how many other urgent cases like mine will there be in the next 2 years? How many other crucial examinations could there possibly be? I don't believe I've harmed anyone; it's quite different from those who damage the National Health Service.

53 State monopolies and dependencies [A]

State, 11:30 on any given day

Beware when you address me, citizens, because I am the State, your State. Yes, the State with a capital "S". I am the synthesis of the fundamental triad of every nation: "territory", "people", and "sovereignty". The Constitution, which forms the foundation of my existence as a State, declares that I care for the citizen. My care is serious, not approximate; loving, not indifferent. I always genuinely care for my people: when it comes to safeguarding all of you, without exception; legislating on health, the safety of workplaces where you carry out your daily tasks, the rules that all of you must respect; protecting every citizen from wars and violence, and punishing those guilty of illegal acts that harm people or property. In essence, my role is clear. I always protect my children from anything that could harm them. My duty is to ensure the safety, well-being, and respect of the citizens. And you, yes, you know perfectly well that I truly care about you; you feel it even when things sometimes don't work as they should. You always know that I am there to hold you close in my arms, you who are my greatest wealth, protecting you adequately. I would never allow anyone to harm you or exploit your assets through means other than institutional ones that are lawful and ethically acceptable. I am trust, reliability, serenity, protection, love. Of course, I am also a vital entity that requires resources to function, but only to provide you, in services, the money that I am obliged to ask for through taxes, and this never changes my course. I always look straight ahead, aiming for the ultimate goal: the happiness and fulfillment of my citizens!

State monopolies and dependencies [B]

State, 11:30 on another random day

I need money, my coffers are empty and I need to replenish them. Something new is needed. In reality, I've tried almost everything, and they've worked! Licenses for thousands of expensive scratch-off tickets that people scratch like chickenpox, from which I take very high percentages. Number draws used to be twice a week, then three times. Then... a crazy idea: allowing lottery draws every 10 minutes. Enough time to satisfy anyone's gambling urge. Just walk into any small-town bar and you'll find hordes of seniors intent on spending their pensions from morning till night! I've managed to collect significant sums, but never enough in a debt-ridden country like ours. I admit, I'm not pleased, but I take a very high percentage from these games without doing practically anything. It's all about gambling addiction! Think about historical football games, betting agencies, and halls where a type of bingo is played. There are many ways to see if Lady Luck is favoring you. Of course, I don't want to create new gambling addicts or undermine the economic health of my citizens. Your safety is my primary concern. But to combat organized crime and illegal gambling, it must be legalized, at least where possible. Isn't my goal a benevolent one? You can see it from the advertising against my own games. Playing responsibly doesn't harm fortunes, doesn't destroy lives and families. If you take a knife, it's up to you whether to use it to cut cheese or to harm yourself. And if that happens, it's certainly not the fault of the knife manufacturer. With my anti-gambling addiction advertising, I warn vulnerable people about the risk of addiction, so the educational aspect is preserved. Cigarettes and tobacco? Same story, right?

54 Tax evasion [A]

Gerlanda, 9:15 on any given day

I am against dishonesty and therefore against any form of tax evasion. Absolutely! In this country, evasion is at very high levels and permeates practically every social stratum, every transaction involving money. Do you realize we are at the top of several rankings listing nations with the highest evasion rates? But then who pays the price for all this? The honest ones like me! It's completely unfair that some citizens break the state's laws by dodging taxes and not paying their dues while others do. Because on the other side there are honest citizens who work hard to earn their daily bread, only to see their paycheck almost halved by the state, which must necessarily bleed them dry due to the lack of other revenues, which are missing precisely because of the evaders. In practice, there are dishonest citizens who earn significant sums that remain untouched because their illegal activities exempt them from taxes, while honest citizens contribute to the functioning of the state, including... for those who are dishonest! Yes, because those dishonest individuals will still use state services, including healthcare, roads, bridges, armed forces, and much more. They will benefit from everything that the state can freely provide to its citizens as its... children, but they will not contribute in any way to the public good. And who will compensate for this shortfall? The others, the honest ones, those who couldn't even cheat if they wanted to, those who see a widening tax gap devouring what they legally earn. It's unjust! I work for two, I'm compensated for two, but I only take home pay for one. These tax evaders should all be identified and heavily punished; the enormous harm they cause to honest people like us, like me, is unforgivable.

Tax evasion [B]

Gerlanda, 7:30 PM on another random day

I brought my car to mechanic Guidello for some major repairs. It's been in the shop for days now, and I'm quite concerned about it. Today, he called me with his usual deep, regretful voice, reminiscent of a doctor delivering news of an incurable illness. He informed me that there's a costly part that needs replacing. Naturally, I inquired about the cost for the replacement part and labor, and he gave me a quote that is so high, it would take me an entire month of work just to pay it off. Seeking alternatives, I asked if there was any possibility to reduce the cost. To my surprise, he suggested that purchasing the part from an alternative market, forfeiting the warranty, paying in cash, and forgoing the invoice could potentially reduce the cost by up to 40%! How could I possibly turn down such a significant saving? I'm fully aware that this isn't fair or ethical, but I earn my money through hard work, unlike those politicians who preach about taxes and combating evasion while comfortably sitting on bank accounts with nine-figure balances. A fluctuation of 40% in repair costs hardly makes a dent in their wealth. For me, however, every penny counts. I've worked diligently to earn my income. Besides, in the grand scheme of tax fraud, evading with this amount pales in comparison to the exorbitant sums the real tax evaders, corporations and successful professionals, defraud from the state. I'm just an honest citizen struggling to make ends meet in the face of rising living costs. When unforeseen expenses like these arise, what choice do I have but to explore viable options to avoid financial ruin? The real evaders are the ones making significant contributions to the black hole that devours me. Reluctantly, I accept the mechanic's proposal. What other choice do I really have?

55 Self-lawmaking [A]

Ascanio, 10:30 on any given day

Politicians are all corrupt, we know that. You don't reach certain positions without getting your hands dirty, without knowing the right people, without skillfully maneuvering in various affairs almost like a mafia boss. Us citizens, on the other hand, are honest and unaware of these mechanisms. Politicians control us, govern us, decide for us without involving us, even though we voted for them. They pursue their own interests and never ours; they only think about themselves. They truly are no good, there's no denying it. A friend of mine, Maldicoro, says they are ultimately just people like us because they come from us. He argues that beasts aren't born from a population where everyone is as good and generous as St. Francis of Assisi, and vice versa. He says that if we are all good, then politicians will be too, but if not, then that self-serving approach is inherent in all of us. Or maybe it's the opportunity that makes a man a thief. I don't buy into Maldicoro's thesis: we are good people, not accustomed to corruption. Can you imagine politicians deciding their own salaries and benefits, and so many other things, through an internal body with judicial powers! It would be impossible for us to behave like that. It's a way of operating typical of politicians and not inherent in honest people like us. However, on one point my friend is right: we talk and complain, but in the end, nothing stops us from trying to enter politics to change things from within. Okay, maybe we made a mistake by not choosing alternatives when we had the chance. We should have had more responsibility towards the public good and brought something good and honest into that world of morally bankrupt individuals. But who knows, maybe it's not too late!

Self-lawmaking [B]

Ascanio, 4:30 PM on another random day

I have to thank my friend Maldicoro who suggested years ago that I should try to pursue a political career. At first, I thought it was impossible, but I gave it a shot. And I succeeded! I started by running in local elections and was elected against all odds. Then, I aimed higher with each subsequent election, striving for more significant positions. Today, I am a respected and esteemed Member of the European Parliament in almost all contexts. Of course, to achieve this, I had to abandon some of the extremism that fueled me at the beginning of this journey. Over time, I learned that being too rigid leads to nothing good, so I moderated myself considerably. Now, many want me to fill various parliamentary influence zones because I try to serve the country's best interests by aligning with the political area whose program matches my beliefs. Oh, I almost forgot… they appointed me president of the internal judicial body that evaluates appeals from parliament employees, namely my colleagues. We're talking about self-legislation here. I gladly accepted! Recently, a group of colleagues filed an appeal requesting salary increases and benefits for several reasons, primarily because our work is very demanding. Also, we are so exposed to corruption attempts from anyone that we cannot afford to receive too low salaries. I convened meetings with my committee, and it wasn't too difficult to decide that my colleague's motion should be approved without many objections. It's nice when things work out smoothly, and everyone agrees on what needs to be done. Yes, of course, the increase also applies to me and all of us on the committee, but this is a side effect of democracy that I cannot avoid in any way!

56 The values of the left-wing [A]

Gaia, 1:00 PM on any given day

I strongly believe in the classic values of the left, and I always have. Before me, my parents believed in them, and I hope that after me, my children will too, provided I manage to pass on my worldview and what deserves to be safeguarded. Social equality must be the primary motive of any party that declares itself leftist. These are the values of ordinary people, of real life, of the individual, and every individual should be respected and supported at all costs, regardless of their social class. It's inconceivable nowadays that there are people so disadvantaged they can't make it to the end of the month, let alone halfway, while on the other side there are people so rich they never have to work another day in their glittering dream lives! It's not fair that people with disabilities don't have easy access to all the services they're entitled to, that they can't even walk down a sidewalk without having to stop after 10 meters. And it's unacceptable that religious minorities face discrimination, that there's homophobia, and that two people of the same sex can't freely kiss in public without sparking a flood of protests from people living in atavistic internal troglodytism. For the rights of these and other minorities, the left must be their standard-bearer! It must represent their bastion of protection. More than that! It must be the entity that, bolstered by the extraordinary empathy typical of activists on this political side, fights for laws to change, minds to change, and society to become modern and progressive, as it should be. The left is the only political force that should hold the fate of the country in its hands, for the good of all.

The values of the left-wing [B]

Gaia, 12:30 PM on another random day

Many have asked me to run on a left-wing list for my municipality. So, I did, and I was elected! From my first electoral victory to my inauguration in Parliament in Rome, it all happened in a flash. I can say I've had a significant political career in a short time! Now, I lead one of the left-wing parties... not the most prominent, certainly, but I can play my part and effect serious change, not like when I was just an ordinary citizen with big dreams and no power. Finally, I can contribute to the leftist cause, but to do so, I must maintain a sufficiently broad political consensus so that no one is too discontented and leaves our camp. But I can do better! By softening our stance on some issues, which perhaps our country isn't quite ready for, I can broaden our base and garner votes from areas that are less leftist but still moderate and progressive! In the end, aside from a few points I don't consider essential right now, our program aligns with that of the opposition. Of course, having 30 out of 31 point is better than having none at all. By postponing the priorities of other points, I can even capture 5% more votes from the center! Politics is also and above all the art of compromise; otherwise, you don't get anywhere. Being too rigid doesn't pay off; it's better to be more inclusive. It's clear that this strategy may cause discontent within my party ranks, but that's par for the course. If it leads to a split, what can I do? Some say it's a loop that repeats itself, that many before me have experienced what I'm going through, and none have managed to stay on the left. But those who talk don't have my responsibilities; they don't know what it means to hold the fate of the party and the country in their hands, to do good for everyone!

57 Belligerent dissonance [A]

Vladimir, 4:00 AM on any given day

Today I, leader of a vast country nostalgic like Prurria, and my powerful and valorous army, have invaded a neighboring sovereign country, Futreania, which has no right to be a country or sovereign at all, but primarily due to its proximity, necessitates intervention to protect our motherland. Yes, I have invaded a sovereign state and I have done so with clear reasons. Futreania once belonged to the territories of my state and then, due to various twists and wars, unjustly gained independence. Well, now I have invaded it. The logical alignment of this so-called independent state with international forces and unions of other countries in the old continent has been a thorn in the side for me and my Prurria for many years. But enough is enough! I have decided: I will raze it to the ground, organize democratic elections, which will surely show a clear preference for my government, and prove that all inhabitants have suffered for years from the separation from our great country and yearn to return to it. Yes, I know there will be thousands of deaths among both military personnel and, unfortunately, civilians. Missiles, bombs, air raids, armies marching, tanks. We will produce complete devastation that will reduce that country to ruins, but only thus can reason prevail once more. Some say my actions hark back to the first half of the twentieth century, a period when the last aspirations of world war were thought to have been relegated, but my reasons have never been considered valid despite my continuous protests. I too regret all those who will fall in this war, which I hope will be as brief as possible, but the necessity to restore the balance disrupted many years ago by independence and recently by this state's alignment with other powers is now a matter of life or death.

Belligerent dissonance [B]

Vladimir, 4:00 PM on another random day

I, Vladimir, president of my great federation, Prurria, have long initiated an extraordinary and necessary military operation in a neighboring country, Futreania, to defend our borders, which were clearly threatened by enemy forces and the likely alliances this country was forging with a wide array of odious capitalist Westerners. My duty as head of state and supreme commander of the armed forces is to protect my country and my citizens! On this, no one can ever say I am not qualified. Today, the dangerous soldiers of the enemy army of Futreania, a country where my army is working to restore international balance, committed an abominable act by blowing up a crucial bridge connecting ours to another friendly state, Slitonia. It's intolerable! This is an abominable act of pure international terrorism that cannot be excused. It is an act of utmost gravity! How could Futreania, which has endangered our motherland Prurria for years, think to attack our sovereign state in such a blatant manner? To brazenly destroy such a vital piece of our international infrastructure? The guilty will pay! Our retaliations will be severe. This is a deliberate attack against freedom, sovereignty, democracy. We will hunt down the perpetrators, judge them, and eliminate them. I know that in this path of rightful vengeance there will be casualties, many casualties, especially on their side, and perhaps civilian victims too, but the reaffirmation of justice requires sacrifices that no one would ever want to make, but which are necessary following provocations of this magnitude. Those who have offended will fall, we will prevail, mark my words, Vladimir!

Gamification 6/10

Paragraph	Only A OR B	Both A AND B
52 The National Health Service	☐ 0 points	☐ 1 point
53 State monopolies and dependencies	☐ 0 points	☐ 1 point
54 Tax evasion	☐ 0 points	☐ 1 point
55 Self-lawmaking	☐ 0 points	☐ 1 point
56 The values of the left-wing	☐ 0 points	☐ 1 point
57 Belligerent dissonance	☐ 0 points	☐ 1 point
TOTAL		

Society

If you think breaking social norms is easy, try getting on a bus and singing at the top of your lungs.

Stanley Milgram

58 Domestic collaboration [A]

Gemma, 2:30 PM on any given day

It is absurd that a woman should still be, even today, the only person in the house to take care of cooking, washing, cleaning, ironing, managing the kids, etc. Where is gender equality in reality? It has been talked about for ages, but in fact, it doesn't exist, starting from the domestic environment, the house, the family, and then extending to work and other areas. A man who equally shares household chores is a chimera, truly, and I am really tired. It seems that the cultural legacy hasn't changed at all over the years. Yes, men talk about equality, they fill their mouths with phrases like 'it's time that...', 'it's right that...', 'it's healthy that...', 'it's modern that...', but then, when they come home, they throw themselves on the couch with the remote control and start the most pointless channel surfing in the universe. And nothing and no one can move them. Convinced that only they have worked, that only they have brought home the bacon, that they are the only ones deserving reverence and services. And us? We work better than them, for the same number of hours, unjustly earning a lower salary, and when we get home we face an extra workload that they don't. And why? Because they were raised and educated by parents who, in perfect adherence to the patriarchal society of the recent past, behaved in the same way. And far from them to evolve, reversing, or better yet, equalizing the tasks! All of this, besides being terribly anachronistic, is absurd! Are we kidding? We are in a society where women have (theoretically) achieved equality that is biologically sanctioned by nature and that only the stupidity of the male has held back for centuries. We are no longer in the Precambrian! It is absolutely normal that men and women have the same tasks and that they share all the activities of daily life. So why doesn't it happen in reality?

Domestic collaboration [B]

Gemma, 10:30 AM on another random day

Today we are guests of our friends, Flusonio and Luigietta. They asked us to arrive a little earlier to help prepare the lunch courses together. As soon as we entered their house, I was taken aback... I saw Flusonio with an apron, busy cleaning the toilet, bidet, sink, and tub in their main bathroom. I am not old-fashioned, but I admit it seems strange to see a big man like him doing such work. Moreover, that troglodyte of my husband Rolfonso, seeing another man doing tasks he would never do, turned purple and green and is experiencing serious embarrassment to the point of not knowing where to look! Yes, because Rolfonso always wants to be in the presence of men who were raised and educated in patriarchal families and who don't want to emancipate themselves. He would never do things like that... everything else is fine, but dishes, bathrooms, laundry, dishwashers... no! Not even under torture, let alone washing the floors and keeping the house in order. After cleaning the bathroom, Flusonio started preparing the pots for lunch. The absurd thing is that Luigietta, instead, is completely relaxed on the couch and occasionally looks after their kids to make sure they don't get hurt while playing. We just finished lunch, and it was really enjoyable. Flusonio, instead of staying seated with us, got up after dessert and started clearing the table, washing, cleaning up, and putting things away, and as much as I am for the equality of tasks, a rule I always reaffirm, it seemed a bit... effeminate! I know it's a paradox for me, who advocates for equality, but that's what I thought. It's okay for a man to help around the house, cook on Sundays, take out the trash, fix things, do the shopping, and many other things, but as a woman, seeing a man cleaning the bathroom feels too strange to me!

59 Etiquette of priority [A]

Oliviero, 4:30 PM on any given day

I've just arrived at Dr. Megaloni's waiting room, a specialist in geriatric prostate exams. I've had this appointment scheduled for months. Megaloni is a renowned figure, and everyone wants to be seen by him! I booked for 6:00 PM, but I arrived much earlier. Upon arrival, the waiting room is already packed. I greet everyone, trying to figure out their appointment times. Others silently speculate about me, giving me scrutinizing looks. Finally, someone starts asking around for information. There are people with appointments after mine! They must be here early because they know it's not about appointment time, but arrival time. It's not fair, obviously, but I don't want to argue; I just want my visit and prescriptions. I've been waiting for 2 hours now, nearing my scheduled visit time and that zone of calm where no one can disturb my wait. At this point, glad I arrived early, I'll manage to leave soon. Suddenly, a patient with an appointment 10 minutes before mine insists on being seen next. I take charge of the rebellion against this outrageous attempt. There he is! The typical Sunday patient ready to argue! If someone has an earlier appointment but arrives last minute, they can't expect to go ahead of those like me who have been waiting all this time! Is that fair? I'm here waiting, and they're out shopping, then they arrive and expect to jump the queue. Absolutely not. Appointment times are clearly just a formality. It's about who arrived first. Sit down and wait your turn, you fool!

Etiquette of priority [B]

Oliviero, 6:30 PM on another random day

Today I booked a new appointment at Dr. Megaloni's office. My appointment is at 6:45 PM, and I'm really at risk of being late today. I shoot out of the office like a rocket and jump into my car. In 10 minutes, I'll be there and hopefully in the waiting room by the scheduled time. Unfortunately, I'll arrive just a few minutes before my appointment time, and if there haven't been too many delays with other afternoon visits, I'll be next when I arrive! Clearly, the agreed-upon time prevails, otherwise what's the point of making this appointment 4 months ago? Well, it's 6:42 PM and I'm entering the waiting room. It's packed as usual. I immediately ask which time slot the doctor is currently seeing and find out there's someone inside who had an appointment immediately before mine, at 6:35 PM. So I loudly assert that I should be next. Some idiot replies that I can't be next because they've been there for 2 and a half hours. I politely ask what time their appointment is, and they tell me it's at 7:30 PM according to their ticket. I retort that they need to wait their turn, otherwise what's the point of scheduling appointments? I'm already annoyed, and my tone of voice makes that clear right away. They're very upset, but I couldn't care less. I have an appointment, and I detest this uncivil habit many have of cutting in line. People need to respect the rules of common living; civility includes this. I have an appointment? Armed with this, I can arrive even at the last moment, and no one can deny me that right. And if someone in the waiting room decides to get up to go in, I wouldn't hesitate to stop them, even forcefully, to assert my right!

60 Alleged culprit: the supermarket [A]

Ida, 10:45 AM on any given day

Every Saturday morning, at the start of the weekend, I'm at the supermarket doing my shopping. It's a relaxing moment after the stress of the workweek. I fill my cart strictly following my list and head to the checkout. I place my items on the black conveyor belt and wait for the cashier to do their job. Ahead of me are 2 customers, one with a large purchase and one with a smaller one. When it's the turn of the customer with the smaller purchase, the anti-theft barrier starts beeping. Instinctively, I glance at the male customer, who immediately puts his hands in his pockets and asks the cashier if the alarm is for him. The cashier, reluctantly but obliged to do his duty, timidly confirms it. The customer starts searching his pockets without pulling anything out... I don't want to insinuate anything, but his behavior seems quite suspicious. Then he opens his wallet, and I start seriously doubting his honesty. I know I shouldn't stare, but I can't help it; I want to see how this unfolds. I briefly turn to the other people in line and raise my eyebrows, met with similar knowing expressions from those who, like me, are observing closely. The customer under scrutiny lifts the bags in his cart, and... voilà! Underneath them appears a pack of lollipops. The customer doesn't have any children with him. It seems to me he intentionally placed it there. He starts mumbling that maybe the lollipops were already there, and the cashier reassures him, saying it was probably just a mistake. But too many things don't add up. I lock eyes again with the customer behind me, who shares my disapproving look about what just happened.

Alleged culprit: the supermarket [B]

Ida, 6:30 PM on another random day

I'm going grocery shopping, like every weekend. Today, I have my 2-year-old son, Tortolino, with me. We wander through the aisles of the enormous supermarket, picking up everything we need for the weekend and the upcoming week when we won't have much time. When we reach the checkout, we greet the cashier who starts scanning the items on the conveyor belt. As soon as I pass through the barriers with the cart, the anti-theft device starts beeping! I'm incredibly embarrassed and look at the cashier, asking if it's our checkout lane's alarm and specifically if it's for me! She nods awkwardly and reassures me, suggesting it might be tags left on our jackets from when we bought them at the respective stores. I quickly defend myself, telling her that I've gone into a thousand other supermarkets with the same jackets and never had any issues. To prove to her that it must have been a mistake, I go back and pass through the barriers again with my son and the empty cart. And... the alarm goes off again, darn it! I meet the smug gazes of the customers behind me. Jerks! I want to tell them that I'm honest and have never stolen anything, even when I could have. But they, mercilessly, continue to stare at me with absolute certainty of my guilt. The cashier keeps telling me I can go in peace, but I'm determined to prove to those idiots behind me that we're innocent. Finally, rummaging through my son's jacket pockets, I find a chocolate bar. What a shame! I start blaming my son's innocence, but I wish I could disappear on the spot. The faces of the other customers begin to express pity for me, as I justify myself, blaming an unaware child.

61 Alleged culprit: the bus [A]

Onofrio, 7:30 PM on any given day

It is 6 PM, and like every day, I get on the bus to go home after work. Today, too, I had a lovely walk from the office to here, but now I'll rest a bit in my warm seat. I take my seat and check my travel pass. After about ten stops, the conductor boards and approaches me to check my ticket. Everything is fine, of course. I'm a super organized person! I follow him with my eyes as he walks away. A little further on, he asks a lady for her ticket, and she, initially distracted, starts to retrieve it from her coat pockets. Then she opens her bag and begins searching clumsily. After several attempts, she sighs in relief and pulls out a ticket from her bag that doesn't look new at all... it's clearly crumpled. She smooths it out a bit with her fingers and hands it to the conductor, who checks it. The ticket has been validated for days, and the conductor politely informs the lady, who begins to justify herself in countless ways. Now... it already seems clear to me that she is one of those people who use public transport without paying and hope to get away with it. I really don't understand how one can exploit public services in this way, which can operate thanks to the ticket that all of us honest people diligently pay for. The conductor has to ask her to pay the ticket on the spot with a surcharge. After a thousand more justifications, the lady pays, insulting the conductor who is simply doing his job correctly. I know I should look away while this is happening, but curiosity to observe someone who dares to board public transport without paying wins out! The other people around me, who are also watching the scene, occasionally look at me, instinctively recognizing me as a decent person like them.

Alleged culprit: the bus [B]

Onofrio, 7:15 AM on another random day

Like every morning, I take the train to work. I have an electronic ticket on my smartphone. The conductor approaches, and with confidence, I pull out my smartphone and proudly display the QR code, with the usual pride that characterizes every tech-immigrant using digital devices. The conductor scans it with his tablet, and while my ears await the usual "thank you and have a nice trip", he coldly tells me that... the ticket is not valid. I blush with embarrassment, smile, and ask... what do you mean? He responds that the ticket is for another date. While the eyes of all the passengers in the carriage turn mercilessly toward me, I check the date and feel reassured. He is wrong; the ticket is for today. I point out that the ticket is for the 16th. He finally acknowledges this but then tells me that today is... the 15th. In an instant, I realize the mistake... it really is the 15th! I have two options: pay the ticket at a higher price or get off at the next stop. Naturally, I choose the former and pay, stammering explanations about my belief that today was the 16th, but from the looks of the passengers, I realize that no one believes me. They all think I'm one of those people who buys a ticket for another day and, if it works out, saves it and then reuses it the next day. If it doesn't, like today, they pay a surcharge. Since the conductor passes by only a few times, there's a lot to gain from it. That's not my case, and I wish I could make everyone relive the moment when I bought the ticket, demonstrating the pure honesty that filled me, but that's impossible. I lower my eyes and continue the journey, hoping my stop comes soon and that no one else gets off with me, forcing me to walk through the underpass in their company of disapproval. The stop arrives. Everyone gets off with me.

62 The soccer match [A]

Iside, 9:00 PM on any given day

I'm watching my beloved team play what might be the most important match of the season. We've already achieved one of our three goals for the year, another one unfortunately fell through, but one remains… the most prestigious: the Citron Cup, coveted by every team on the planet! I really hope we can celebrate a well-deserved victory. The game has been played with utmost mutual respect, at least until now. But no, darn it! During a counterattack that was working perfectly, completely catching the opposing midfield off guard, our forward is brutally brought down by the last defender before the goalkeeper. The goal was certain! The trip is blatant; the opposing defender clearly aimed for the legs, not the ball! I watch the replay several times, and the scene becomes increasingly dramatic to my eyes, almost gruesome. My god, I can only imagine the pain! Our player goes airborne and then lands in a chaotic roll, and the opponent falls on him, worsening the situation! It almost seems like he's piling on in the fall. Terrible! Absolutely a red card offense! Now the referee will surely give a just punishment to the opponent who gets up and blatantly explains he did nothing. Ours is on the ground, clutching his leg in terrible pain. And finally, the referee... the referee... WHAT? NO! How can this be? Simulation and a yellow card for our player? This is ABSURD! The opponent almost killed him! How can such a wrong judgment be made? Are we crazy? Come on! It's clear this referee has something against us and is favoring the other team. Hopefully, VAR will intervene. What? I can't believe it! Even VAR confirms there was no foul? Then it's a conspiracy!

The soccer match [B]

Iside, 9:50 PM on the same random day

It's the second half. The game is fast-paced and energetic, a true spectacle to witness the competitive action of our players. Right now, the opposing team is attacking, and unfortunately, one of their forwards has managed to slip through our midfielders and is heading towards our goal! Our defender crosses paths with the forward, who has entered the penalty area, in an exemplary manner, and then... suddenly, he dramatically falls to the ground. Oh no! What are you trying to achieve? Come on! The player grimaces in pain as if our defender had struck him, but it's absolutely false, he didn't even touch him, it's evident! They were almost 3 meters apart when they collided! The attacker is clearly diving; we hope the referee doesn't fall for it because it's an outrageous farce! Now even the stretcher is coming out to increase the psychological pressure on the referee who has to decide whether to award a penalty or not. I watch and re-watch the video multiple times and see no foul committed by our player. He executed a normal defensive maneuver without harming the opposing attacker, who exaggeratedly flew into the air and then to the ground. The referee consults via radio, pulls out a yellow card, and points to the penalty spot. Are we kidding? He didn't even touch him! Everyone saw it! It's a clear simulation! I hope they invoke VAR. They do! We're saved! Everyone waits for the final judgment. What? The penalty is confirmed? Are we crazy? It's clear the referee is biased towards the opposing team, you don't need a fortune teller to see that. Every decision he makes is against us, always in favor of the opponents. It's absurd that matches with bought-off refereeing are still permissible nowadays! It's truly intolerable, unsportsmanlike, criminal!

63 Children and interference [A]

Orlanda, 10:45 AM on any given day

I made it on my own... entirely! I didn't receive any help or push, nor any recommendations, ever. Yet, I managed... to build a life, to find a good job, to start a family. That's why I firmly believe that children should grow and mature by themselves, as much as possible. They need to learn to stand up for themselves independently, without any interference. They should indeed embrace their parents' teachings in terms of ethics, respect, and morality, but above all, they must learn to apply them without parental intervention. Parents should be supportive, yes, but not more than that. Experiences, conflicts, even quarrels (as long as they're skirmishes and not dangerous aggressions), contribute to shaping our children's characters. Girls and boys need to train themselves, create their emotional spectrum on their own! Parents can gently guide them, indicating what's right and wrong, perhaps pointing out limits not to exceed, but they shouldn't meddle in their little disputes because by doing so, they don't allow their inherent defense capabilities to grow, mold, structure, and react. And come on! At the end of the day, they're children! How can a parent interfere in these tiny squabbles that can only be formative in the end? How can we judge skirmishes over things like who owns a piece of candy or the right to use a ball for a bit? When I read messages in the class chat from parents accusing, defending, blaming, or getting upset over a word said to their child by a classmate, I try to extinguish all fires by saying that they're just children after all, and we should let them be free to get offended and clash, so that they can also develop a capacity for self-defense that should not and must not depend on intrusive parents.

Children and interference [B]

Orlanda, 2:30 PM on another random day

Today, my son Vulrico came to me and shared that he had been called a "slacker" by his friend Pludemio. I was taken aback. Vulrico looked deeply hurt, unable to respond. My heart sank seeing him like this. I reassured him that he's a hard-working boy who simply needs a bit more encouragement in his studies. Yet, the sting of those words lingered. I decided to address this directly. First, I'll have a word with Pludemio's parents. It's important they understand the impact of such words on Vulrico's self-esteem. Then, I'll speak with his teacher and the school principal. It's not just about defending my son's honor; it's about ensuring fairness and respect in the school environment. I took action immediately, posting in the moms' chat group about what happened. Some tried to down-play it, suggesting it's just kids being kids. But "slacker" isn't just a playful jab… it's hurtful and demeaning. Vulrico is any-thing but lazy; he's enthusiastic and eager to learn when prop-erly guided. I can't help but wonder where Pludemio picked up such language. It's concerning if it reflects his home environ-ment. Regardless, I won't let Vulrico be labeled unfairly. He deserves better than baseless insults from peers who may not understand the impact of their words. My husband and I work tirelessly to provide a bright future for Vulry. He's not just our son; he's a proactive, resilient young boy who deserves respect. I won't rest until this matter is addressed appropriately. It's about standing up for Vulrico and ensuring every child feels safe and valued in school, free from unwarranted judgments.

64 The horoscope [A]

Lorena, 10:35 AM on any given day

I have been fortunate and have had the desire to study, a lot. Now I am an established professional; I believe in science, in everything that is tangible, demonstrable, true. I absolutely do not believe in the nonsense that many believe in. I don't understand how some people can swallow phenomena that are absolutely unprovable or theories that have nothing verifiable, nothing credible, nothing solid at their core. I am a steadfast woman, not gullible at all; I am well-versed in many subjects and consider myself an absolute devotee of competence, science, and understanding, wherever possible, of all phenomena. I read a lot, study a lot. In short, I'm not easily fooled! Sometimes I read incredible posts by unknown authors on social media and laugh at the idea that anyone could believe such non-sense. It's not about fake news, mind you; these are just crazy theo-ries, surreal conspiracy hypotheses. If someone writes that donkeys fly, but does so grammatically and syntactically correctly and per-haps gives a journalistic appearance to their text, well, that someone starts receiving dozens and dozens of comments from people who agree with what was stated. It's a shame that those theories are com-pletely false and refuting them is child's play, but under the post, an increasingly large number of pleased people begin to gather, saying things like "I generally don't believe in these things, but in this case, there must be something true because this gentleman claims that sightings of flying donkeys number in the thousands every day, so surely they are hiding something from us." And then at some point, I see among the comments, there are some from friends whom I re-spected, and my opinion of them drastically falls... How can they swallow these tall tales?

The horoscope [B]

Lorena, 12:30 PM on another random day

I'm having lunch with my colleagues and we're chatting pleasantly. At one point, I notice certain traits in Sigmondo's character that I believe can be associated with a specific zodiac sign. I don't really believe in these things, but the characterization of people born in the same period is often unmistakable. I ask him for his birth month because I'm almost convinced he belongs to a particular zodiac sign, as people from that sign often exhibit very distinct characteristics. He replies telling me he's from the "Cimaduolo" sign, but he absolutely doesn't believe in anything related to the zodiac or horoscopes. Surprised, I tell him I thought he was from the "Poraccio" sign or at least the "Guorino" sign, as they share many characteristics with "Cimaduolo". He insists he's from "Cimaduolo". I don't give up and ask for his birth day and month. He tells me, and this confirms the oddity... he really is from "Cimaduolo"! Weird. Perhaps being born on the cusp between signs explains it, but yes, that must be it! He reiterates that he doesn't believe at all that the projection of stars from different and distant galaxies onto the celestial vault of planet Earth, arbitrarily associated with names of animals or whatever else, could possibly influence anyone's character. Furthermore, since there are only 12 zodiac signs, he cannot accept the idea that every day 1/12th of the world's population would have the same description. I reply that I too am highly skeptical in general and hardly believe in horoscopes, sometimes consulting them just for fun. However, when it comes to zodiac signs related to birth times, well, there are undeniable truths there. Call it atmosphere, if you will, but people born in the same period often have similar characteristics!

65 Superstition [A]

Osvaldo, 8:45 AM on any given day

I'm a man of the kind that no mold has ever held. I owe nothing to anyone, and it can be said that I made myself. I've created, practically from nothing, relying solely on my intuition, a small empire. I'm one of those who studied hard to become what I am today. I believe in ideas, in projects, in entrepreneurship, in pragmatism. And I'm endowed with great rationality and common sense. I believe in everything that is verifiable, demonstrable, real. By the way, market laws work relentlessly like this! If the product you offer is something that end users really need, then you will sell it without any problem! But if the product is just a whim of yours and has no connection to the daily needs of ordinary people, well, then you won't go anywhere. When I hear some entrepreneurs, especially young ones, I realize that their certainties are based on ideas that are up in the air. The only law that wins is the law of the market. If you sell, you succeed; if you don't sell... no, it's straightforward! There are also fellow entrepreneurs of mine who have fetishes, superstitious trinkets that they carry with them from the outset, thinking that in them lies the strength or luck that propels them. I don't believe at all in such nonsense. This is pure superstition. And I read so much nonsense based on these popular beliefs. I don't understand how people can believe things like those that circulate, even before the web, among people, remnants of popular beliefs from the past. There's nothing possible in these illusory theories. I am a person of integrity, not a gullible one; I am well-informed on many subjects. I've said it before: I consider myself a devotee of culture and truth in all phenomena. I read a lot, study a lot. In short, I'm not easily fooled!

Superstition [B]

Osvaldo, 4:10 PM on another ordinary day

I summoned a colleague to my office to discuss an important project. We delved deeply into all the issues and everything is clear. However, the project is complex, mainly due to the client's lack of clarity. My colleague, with an air of condescension, told me that if things were to go wrong, well, we won't exactly die on this project. Why talk about death? What does that have to do with anything? Why evoke the demise of the project, the company, or ourselves as human beings? Honestly, I've always detested this kind of talk... I don't like it at all! I smiled at him and somewhat subtly, I placed my hands near my intimate parts in an apotropaic gesture that our ancestors used to do when a funeral procession passed by. Yes, we're in the office, which can be considered a public setting, surrounded by colleagues, but I did it discreetly enough to make my colleague understand that certain things are better left unsaid. The future of the project is too important, not to mention the value of the company. I know these gestures serve absolutely no purpose; I'm not foolish, but in doubt, it's better to ward off any risk. What harm does it do? He, not satisfied, downplayed my gesture by telling me that nothing and no one is ever completely safe because in life, anything can happen at any moment. Darn it, this pessimism continues! I put my hands in the pockets of my jacket draped over the chair's backrest and found the car keys which I touched. It also serves no purpose, but who knows... what harm does it do? I certainly don't need to sacrifice a lamb on the altar to change the favor of the gods; I just need to touch myself a bit and grasp some iron in my hands. I don't have any other superstitious gestures, except when salt spills or oil is spilled, but that's another story.

66 Individual and crowd ^A

Leo, 10:30 AM on any given day

I love the individuality of each of us and at the same time, I love the group that brings together multiple people. I certainly love the freedom that each individual has, the differences of each person, and the strength of everyone. But at the same time, I cannot deny that I love the multiplied, hundredfold strength of a group of individuals working together, playing together, or even just experiencing a moment of joy or passion together. Whether it's a game at the stadium, a rock concert, or something as significant as a street protest to assert one's or others' rights. All of this is wildly human, sweetly and empathetically human! Feeling hearts beating in unison, diverse in origin, culture, personal history, and yet all equal, all oriented towards a common goal, is wonderful! No, I'm not afraid to be amidst vast crowds at the stadium and feel together the thrill at the start of our favorite band's most successful song. It's something that literally gives me goosebumps. You're there and you're moved, and tens of thousands of other people feel, if not the exact same emotion, something very, very similar. It's hard to describe unless you experience it directly at least once in your life. And then, shall we talk about common passions? Or widespread activities like going out in the morning for a jog and meeting other people doing the same? Smiling at them as if you've known them for a lifetime even though it's the first time you've met? Taking your dog out and meeting others doing the same, knowing intimately that they share the same respect for animals? Going to an exhibition of a famous painter and finding yourself in ecstasy in front of a piece of art with others who, in silence, are sharing the same emotion? Unique...!

Individual and crowd [B]

Leo, 4:30 PM on another ordinary day

It was absurd, on Saturday I went to the exhibition fair in my city, and it was a nightmare! Thousands of cars lined up, buses packed with people like sardines, endless lines at the ticket office, endless lines at the entrance (and I wonder why we need two lines when we could enter directly after getting the ticket), biblical queues to enter the pavilions, and epic queues just to use the bathrooms! I won't tell you what we had to do to buy a beer and a sandwich... after getting the ticket with the number, we waited almost half an hour... inconceivable! I'm not talking about the fair itself, which rightly is experiencing a moment of great success, and that's fine. I'm talking about the people, the crowd. What sense does it make to cram in like this? What sense does it make for everyone to rush to the fair on the same day?! But come on, you all know that Saturdays are chaotic, especially the first and even more the last day! But did everyone have to come here today to ruin our day? No, well, people are stupid, from every point of view. They choose the same time for every phase of the day. They crowd into the same areas at the same time instead of spreading out better. Of course, I couldn't do otherwise because today was my only free slot, but what about the others? Shall we talk about the others? And anyway, the morning didn't start any better. This morning I woke up early, really early, like at 5:00. I put on my tracksuit and sneakers and decided to go to the self-service car wash to clean my utility vehicle. I arrived expecting to be the only one at that hour, but instead... I found two other people already there washing their cars. Do you really have nothing better to do? Why not stay asleep at that hour? Bah, I find it truly absurd. I detest crowds!

67 Nepotism and family [A]

Ottavio, 10:30 AM on any given day

I introduced my daughter Piderolia to the boss! No hidden corporate agenda, mind you, but... who knows. She's really keen on that assistant professor position, and my boss holds sway over the university bigwigs. He can certainly ensure her application gets, well, not pushed forward, but at least considered! In that circle, getting the big shot professor to cast a merciful eye her way is like acing the selections! My boss has surely understood; I don't need to ask him anything, he already knows what to do. After all, he owes it to me for the great work I do at the company, assisting him in everything. I don't think I'm harming anyone this way. What's wrong with introducing someone to someone else so they can simply assess their skills, quick thinking, coherence of thoughts, and why not, even their beauty. Let me be clear, I know this isn't something to push with my boss, but today my daughter is flaunting some wonderful hair. She's already a beautiful girl, but right now she's glowing. Anyway, it would be beneficial if my boss got to know her a bit more. I'm saying this for the good of the company, of course... it would be advantageous for all of us if the managers noticed what Piderolia is made of. Suppose her university career turns out to be a disappointment or at least not very lucrative, a managerial position here wouldn't be bad. She absolutely has all the qualifications to handle even the most complex of jobs. I know my colleagues also yearn for such positions for their children, but I have a sort of implicit first right. I can use my influence with the company management to highlight a truly outstanding talent to them. I'm not selling a fake; I'm doing what I can solely for the benefit of whoever hires my daughter!

Nepotism and family [B]

Ottavio, 4:30 PM on another day

The well-connected is one of the most infamous beings in the known universe. Infamous him, those who recommend him, and those who support that recommendation by carrying out unjust, illegal, and detrimental practices to others. I have had an open case for years at the National Institute for Lost Causes and I cannot get it examined in any way. Surely this happens because others' dossiers pass ahead of mine thanks to the saints in heaven of the bearer. How annoying, how angry! I deeply hate this way of doing things, I hate recommendations. I feel disgust towards those who use tricks to get ahead of others. I detest those who, with all sorts of excuses, skip lines or who arrive at a doctor's office, or any other office, and after exchanging a few words with the secretary, go straight in ahead of everyone else. I scorn those who, knowingly causing most of the problems in any public entity due to what he and only he considers an urgency, call the friend of a friend and jump to the top of the list, managing to have their cases examined very quickly, disregarding all the others who are nobody's children. People who don't hesitate to bend over backwards to talk to the school principal so that their child ends up in a section that is not considered the least snobby in the institute. The true decay of society is right here! And then we complain about delays, endless waiting lists, injustices! The same people who abuse and ask for recommendations, if you catch them at the bar, they speak badly of the so-called recommended ones, to whom they themselves belong. It's intolerable to hear them speak like that even though you know that just a few days before they used their petty connections solely to avoid waiting even one more day for matters of their personal interest.

68 Privacy protection [A]

Letizia, 6:00 PM on any given day

It's absurd, but it's happened again! They listen to me, they spy on me, they persecute me! How is it possible that the Flofle search engine already knows what I want to buy?! It's watching us! I don't know what services are active on my smartphone without my knowledge, but every time I search for something on the search engine, maybe on my phone, then I'm inundated with offers for similar products, for days, for weeks, and wherever I connect, whatever site I browse, I see banners, boxes, notifications everywhere related to the boots I desire and searched for days ago. This happens to me very often while browsing the Internet, and it only ends if I finally buy that product or stop making similar searches for several months. It's as if they exploit my momentary desire to detect my vulnerability and use it until I decide to get rid of that desire by finally purchasing the coveted product. But how do they do it? Who authorizes them to use my data? This is surely illegal! No one can spy on what I do on the web without my permission, but then, how can they be everywhere? On the phone, on the computer, on the smart TV? It's mind-boggling, I feel spied on, observed, illegally monitored in every move I make on the web, in every choice I want to make. There's always this sort of big digital brother ready to suggest this or that, and always, I mean always, starting from my recent search. I've talked about this with friends who tell me they experience the same phenomenon and similar things happen to them too. This is intolerable. It's really a violation of personal privacy, aimed at the profit of some tech giants who want to shamelessly exploit my tastes and passions by openly violating my privacy. This is something to report, something for a class action lawsuit!

Privacy protection [B]

Letizia, 2:00 PM on another day

My friend Protonia suggested a new service from Flofle that is truly phenomenal! It's called Flofle Suite. I tried it and instantly fell in love with it. Why? Well, first of all, because it's free, and it's incredible that such a comprehensive and powerful tool is free! I can't thank Protonia enough for this amazing tip. Just think, I can send generous-sized emails without paying a cent, create and publish videos, write text documents, spreadsheets, create forms, databases, presentations, draw maps, use many apps on my smartphone, the navigator, chat with artificial intelligence, and all without spending a penny! Flofle has made this strategy its strength; imagine that now more than 2 billion people use its services! It really makes you wonder how they manage to maintain all these huge and expensive infrastructures, but if they do it, they must surely have their good reasons. That's not my concern, though; what matters to me is using the tools. I'm very curious and love trying innovative services, so as soon as Protonia sent me the link to the suite, I rushed to my PC and clicked with great curiosity. I immediately saw a page describing the new service, stating that it would be free forever. One more click, and I signed up! I filled in all the required fields, entered my email and desired password, then ticked off a lot of checkboxes in a very long list — the usual huge page that nobody ever reads because it's too long and boring — and finally, with another long text labeled 'license agreement', I clicked 'accept' and 'next' 3 or 4 times. In the end, I was ready to start using this new wonder! And now, honestly, I really can't do without it anymore!

69 Africa and raw materials [A]

Pio, 10:00 AM on any given day

I wrote a thesis on European companies in Africa. It was a really interesting project. I admit I've never been particularly attentive to these matters, so this opportunity taught me a lot. I didn't know that hundreds of companies were established in Africa, many of which belong to my own country. It's incredible; we extract everything in Africa... Searching the web reveals that many of the raw materials that "power" what we call the West come from there! Our companies extract oil, natural gas, copper, petroleum, diamonds, gold, iron, bauxite, coal, titanium, uranium, etc., in Africa. They produce in Africa and then import coffee, cotton, cocoa, tea, rubber, etc., to our continent. And it doesn't end there... there's a mineral that is essential for the production of digital devices and is present in our smartphones, in fact, in every smartphone on the planet, and that's coltan! The largest coltan mines are in the Democratic Republic of Congo, which is also one of the world's largest producers. There are many companies, and there's a lot of competition among European (and non-European) countries to secure a share of those resources. Fortunately, Africa is vast, so there's enough for everyone. If the flow of raw materials we retrieve from Africa were to suddenly stop one day, it would cripple many of our multinational corporations. Oh, and of course, there are companies that bring raw materials from Africa to Europe without much regard for the country of origin, paying workers ridiculously low wages and ignoring tax issues, so their wealth grows disproportionately and unfairly. But what can we do? In short, from the perspective of raw materials, Africa is perhaps the... world's foremost power!

Africa and raw materials [B]

Pio, 2:30 PM on the same day

I can't stand these illegal immigrants anymore! They keep landing on our shores from Africa without documents, permits, authorizations, visas. Do they even know that this is a sovereign state? With laws and regulations that must be respected, otherwise there's jail or worse? I can't even stand those who come legally from Africa to steal our jobs. Seriously... you have all that wealth in Africa, why come here to take what belongs to us? We were born on this territory and fortunately it's rich in resources that are meant for us to exploit. You surely have your own resources, right? Go away, you can't use ours. Enough, we need to do something, like preventing them from arriving! Have you ever seen, in a normal world, citizens of one state going to another state to exploit its wealth, entering a place that doesn't belong to them to consume its resources? We're talking about resources that have always been there and rightfully belong to that country and its people! The wealth is ours and we're keeping it. And then... all that money to keep them in reception centers, do we realize how much these expenses damage us? For me, everyone out! No one can consume what belongs to us for their own benefit. This exploitation must stop! Go back to your homes and keep your hands off our property! Look for work in your own land so rich in resources! You're crazy if, with all that wealth, you don't bother to start businesses to exploit it.. I really don't understand, you should be very wealthy and yet you don't feel like doing anything, and just to avoid working you take a boat risking your lives, cross our common sea, and come here to squander our money shamelessly. This is pure and simple exploitation!

70 Intellectual property [A]

Teobaldo, 10:00 AM on any given day

I'm a creative musician; I love making original music by playing various instruments. I enjoy using sampled loops, producing albums, shooting and editing videos, and publishing them on my web channels... and why not, even earning something from it. I've also written and published several books on the subject. It's truly satisfying to see the number of views or downloads grow! Unfortunately, just like in the physical world, there are always people who steal in the digital world too! Often, I find parts of my work in others' without any credit given. Could it be that they've written an identical piece? Yes, it's possible, but finding snippets of my videos in other videos without any reference to me? No, this can't be random in the slightest! My music is used as soundtracks without earning me anything, unlike when they are published on my channels. In short, it's really difficult to protect the work of one's creativity! Protecting myself? Of course, I've done that; now, everything is under license, and I've deposited the tracks, videos, and creations with organizations dedicated to their protection. Certainly, those who want to reproduce them can do so without problems, and I'll earn something. But those who want to use them must request my authorization and pay royalties. And if they refuse to pay? No need to go to court; just notifying the organization initiates the obligation for removal, deletion, or modification of the fruits of my labor from their publications. It's only fair! It's absolutely wrong to illegally exploit others' creative work for profit without rightfully compensating those who put in the creative effort. It's outright theft and should be treated as such. If you pay royalties, well, you're welcome!

Intellectual property [B]

Teobaldo, 11:00 AM on another day

Yesterday my favorite band released a new album and I can't wait to listen to it. It's been at least 4 years since their last album, and the anticipation has become unbearable. Now I'm itching with excitement to hear it. Although their previous album wasn't as extraordinary as their earlier works, so I hope this one will be good... They've chosen young and inspired producers, and they've taken a long time to produce it. Come on, it will probably be a good piece of work! But, but... What if I don't like it? Even today, a full album from a top-notch band costs quite a bit. I don't want to spend all that money on something that I might not like or that could be so forgettable that even if I like it, I could forget it within half a day. I want to listen to it before buying it. Yes, I know I can use the free streaming of short previews of each song, but I get annoyed by the ads or the fact that I can't control the playlist. I also know there are monthly subscriptions that cost very little and remove ads while giving you listening freedom, okay, but why pay that money when I can have the same things for free by listening to the album beforehand without spending a dime? I'm not stupid. I've said it and I'll say it again, the prices of these products are still too high. Anyway, I'm dying to listen to it. You know what I'll do? I'll go on peer-to-peer networks and download the album for free. But no, I'm not doing anything wrong. Want to compare me to those who do it for a living? Who profit from it? And besides, I want to download one album, not 200 albums and 400 films. Those are the ones committing a crime. I'll listen to it, and if it lives up to their historic works, if I really like it, I'll probably buy it. I have the right to know in detail what I'm buying before purchasing, right?

71 Society and migrants - I ^A

Prisco, 9:45 AM on any given day

Today I heard on TV that the phenomenon of gangmastering is assuming increasingly large dimensions. Gangmastering is the exploitation of low-cost labor that circumvents labor laws and regulations. It is now universally widespread, wherever there are agricultural productions or significant livestock farming, of course. The way these workers are treated is terrible, often undocumented immigrants seeking shelter and a daily meal. They work in terrible conditions, under the sun or rain, with prolonged hours beyond all reason, without breaks, pauses, rest, without any protection or safety. And often they also become seriously ill. And some of them lose their lives! It's terrible, I imagine, to be in a foreign country you've reached hoping to make a fortune and end up working exploited in the most atrocious way, in global indifference. And then to fall ill without anyone caring for you, left in a shack feeling like a burden that won't bring anything home those days. And then to die without anyone knowing, and perhaps being discarded somewhere to pass off death as accidental death. Gangmastering is widespread in agriculture, livestock farming, but also in other areas such as construction. And it's not just in the south, mind you; it's widespread across the entire territory and in all states. How can we escape from this situation of semi-slavery? I have no idea. And if one of these poor souls tried to rebel by shining a light on what is happening to him and his brothers, he would quickly come to a bad end. Gangmastering is run by unscrupulous people who aren't afraid to commit terrible acts. It's not possible that in the modern era we live in, such things still happen, that there are still episodes of labor exploitation like this; something must be done!

Society and migrants - I [B]

Prisco, 6:00 PM on another day

Wow, today I went grocery shopping and my trusted supermarket didn't have the PDO Matured Magenta Tomatino from Lower Stùrfia anymore. It's a truly delicious and irreplaceable product that costs very little! There are intensive cultivations of this small tomato all over the country, and many people work along its supply chain. My favorite tomato supports many livelihoods, so it's absurd that it's not available today! I immediately asked the seller why this serious shortage had occurred, and he told me there have been protests among the workers who harvest it. It seems they work under less than dignified conditions. How can harvesting fresh produce in the fields, even with a few extra hours, be undignified? I wonder if people today still know what it means to work, to break their backs to bring home bread! No, they don't! They don't know what I had to do to secure a dignified position that allows me to choose what to eat. Today I want my tomato, and it's not normal that I can't have it. I pay, and by paying, I always want to be satisfied and take home what I intended to buy. And the prices? Shall we talk about the prices? Why has the price of a tray of normal tomatoes increased by 5%? Now they cost 1.05 €/kg! What could possibly be so expensive about ten tomatoes harvested from a tree? I come to the discount store to pay less, not to find surprises like this. They were advertised at €1 in the flyer, so now I demand to pay €1 for them! Damn it, I had even planned a dinner with Rafiòla, the girl I like, and I wanted to cook her a dish of delicious spaghetti with Stùrfia tomatoes, and now I can't do it. They'll hear from me at the higher levels of the supermarket; I've been a customer for years!

72 Social network - I ^A

Luisa, 5:30 PM on any given day

Whether we like it or not, social networks are now an important part of everyone's life. Whether we like it or not, they hold more value than attending a conference, more than an electoral speech, and unfortunately, sometimes even more than a gathering with friends at a pizzeria. Many people are influenced by the opinions expressed in the posts of illustrious strangers who become millionaires without any plausible reason! And in doing so, the viewpoints of a few, perhaps the most foolish, become global opinions through the power of likes... I wonder, what authority do these individuals have to sway the ideas of the masses? I really don't know... I believe that before believing every piece of news, one should verify the credibility of the sources that produced it. There are no true or false news stories in themselves, but it's clear that news from well-known and authoritative sources, such as major news outlets or television programs, will have been verified in detail many times over. The companies behind these headlines value their reputation and cannot afford any slip-ups by spreading fake news. Publishing a news story that is later debunked would mean losing credibility and the trust of readers, leading to a decline in success and ultimately financial loss. As a result, news stories are thoroughly scrutinized! Everything must be verified: places, people, times. Analysis is conducted on every sentence, every statement. As readers, we trust major journalistic outlets when they report something, and we trust even more when multiple reputable sources corroborate the same news, or as they say, "rebat it.". We shouldn't be gullible; we should be attentive, shrewd!

Social network - I [B]

Luisa, 5:30 PM on another day

Today I came across a series of news on some social media platforms that left me quite bewildered. For example, I read on Fakebook that if you eat walnuts after drinking orange soda, you risk collapsing. It seems there is a significant interaction between the flavonoids in nuts that pair with the surfactants from residues of melon peel sometimes found in orange peels. Yes, it may sound strange, but thinking about it, the other day after Sunday lunch at my sister's house, my son felt unwell with severe stomach pains. He loves orange soda and as usual had some from a can that my sister, as always, kindly provided. After lunch, we also ate some nuts, and he had a few walnuts. Is it true? I don't know, but from today onwards, I will avoid this combination. It's odd that there are no indications about orange soda or walnuts, but anyway, better to be cautious. I also delved into it by searching on the search engine I use and found that another social network, Ittiogram, claims this happens because watermelon processing is done simultaneously with oranges due to illegal international trafficking of artificial pollen produced by North Scaptkandian bees. Well, now things actually start to make sense! If this happens in reality, then who knows what germs our vegetables and fruits are contaminated with. And then the orange soda... Binperestic says that products from powerful multinational companies like this beverage certainly do not benefit our health. It talks about harmful products and states that it's absurd to risk our health for them! These are unscrupulous companies whose only goal is profit and they have no respect for us as end-users!

73 Dream of living in the countryside - II [A]

Raimondo, 1:15 PM on any given day

I can't stand the city stress anymore... the traffic, the noise, the endless things to do, the crowds everywhere. Enough! I need to disconnect, to go live in a place of absolute tranquility, maybe in the countryside, isolated from everything and everyone. I need to regenerate myself, find myself again, the calm, the serenity, the joy of living. I need slow, unhurried times. I don't want to face the thousand burdens that life imposes on me every day, to go from one commitment to another as if there were no tomorrow, just to come home exhausted in the evening, spend a night that seems shorter than a blink, and wake up at dawn to face another daunting day. I want the countryside, the mountains, the sea, a chalet in the middle of nowhere, on a hill, in a valley, anywhere surrounded by nature, where I can hear the sounds of animals and water flowing in a nearby river. The birdsong, the whisper of the wind. I need to disconnect. And then, work. I really can't take it anymore! Sometimes I wish I could get sick, break a leg and be forced to stay home for days. Only then could I have a break, relax a bit amidst all this breakdown. I have so many passions that I never have time to devote myself to. If I finally had the chance to stay at home, I would dedicate myself to painting, music, crocheting, DIY projects, fixing this and that, and many, many other things. Time passes too quickly, I can't hold onto anything, I can't enjoy anything. Everything is fast, elusive, accelerated. The days fly by in front of my eyes like an F1 car in front of the grandstands, and it's a race towards death. Tonight I'll close my eyes, reopen them, and I'll already be old, on the verge of the grave. What kind of life is this? I need to pull the handbrake!

Dream of living in the countryside - II [B]

Raimondo, 4:45 PM on another day

I've been in the countryside for quite some time now and I can't take it anymore. Firstly, it's absurd that there's no internet connection here, what year are we living in? I can't communicate with anyone effectively. How am I supposed to keep up with all my activities? I'll complain to the owner about this. And then, can you believe I have to wash with cold water because the heating often doesn't work? Sometimes the power goes out, can you imagine? What kind of power plants are they using here, ones from the 1800s? Do you know what kind of damage this does to my notebook... And this fresh cow's milk. How can I drink it if it's not provided in a proper container? I risk getting sick, getting an infection. Sure, it's a beautiful place, but I never expected this when I arrived here... just 24 hours ago! I can't stand the stagnation, the boredom anymore. I need to get out, see my friends in person, engage in any kind of activity. Ironically, I miss work a lot. How can anyone stay locked up at home for so long? I can't take this situation anymore. And then, there's nothing to do here, nothing interesting, no activities that can really engage me, not even Blastfix! It's like being imprisoned, time never passes, it moves at an agonizing slowness. Okay, it's true, in the past I've always dreamed of slowing down, but this is too much. Every day feels like a month away from here, I count the hours, the minutes, the seconds. And they never pass, never. I have no commitments, no deadlines. I could devote myself to activities I've always put aside, that's true, but honestly, I have no desire to! I don't know why, I can't explain it. Maybe a middle ground between a hectic life and an immobile life would be preferable to this stagnation. Yes, that's what I should long for now, a life that balances stress, frenzy with calm and relaxation!

Gamification 7/10

Paragraph	Only A OR B	Both A AND B
58 Domestic collaboration	☐ 0 points	☐ 1 point
59 Etiquette of priority	☐ 0 points	☐ 1 point
60 Alleged culprit: the supermarket	☐ 0 points	☐ 1 point
61 Alleged culprit: the bus	☐ 0 points	☐ 1 point
62 The soccer match	☐ 0 points	☐ 1 point
63 Children and interference	☐ 0 points	☐ 1 point
64 The horoscope	☐ 0 points	☐ 1 point
65 Superstition	☐ 0 points	☐ 1 point
66 Individual and crowd	☐ 0 points	☐ 1 point
67 Nepotism and family	☐ 0 points	☐ 1 point
68 Privacy protection	☐ 0 points	☐ 1 point
69 Africa and raw materials	☐ 0 points	☐ 1 point
70 Intellectual property	☐ 0 points	☐ 1 point
71 Society and migrants - I	☐ 0 points	☐ 1 point
72 Social network - I	☐ 0 points	☐ 1 point
73 Dream of living in the countryside - II	☐ 0 points	☐ 1 point
TOTAL		

Love and sexuality

I asked my wife, "On a scale of 1 to 10, what rating would you give me as a lover?" She replied, "You know I'm not good with fractions".

Rodney Dangerfield

74 Pansexuality [A]

Martinello, 6:00 PM on any given day

The evening news reported yet another act of discrimination against a same-sex couple. How can there still be people behaving in such a discriminatory way? How is it possible to still harbor such prejudices in this day and age? The world has evolved for millennia, we're not in the Middle Ages anymore, come on! I have nothing against homosexuality, how could I? If it's true that everyone is free to do as they please as long as it doesn't infringe upon the freedom of others, then surely they are free to love whoever they choose, including someone of the same sex. But really, what do these idiots care about who I love? Moreover, if I write on social media about being crazy about painting and particularly about a painting, no one criticizes me; in fact, I'm seen as cool! If I express love for animals, I'm viewed as extremely sensitive with a big heart. But if I post a photo of two same-sex lovers, I get attacked! How can anyone think they can restrict those feelings for which human beings should be as free, natural, and happy as possible, namely attraction, desire, passion? Everyone should be able to love whomever they want without any limits, thus ensuring maximum freedom of expression of feelings. Of course! If I kiss my girlfriend in public, why shouldn't two men or two women do the same? What madness is it to exalt modesty, public respect for something that is absolutely innate? How can my personal attraction to the opposite sex have more dignity than an attraction to the same sex? In the end, we are all somewhat pansexual. We experience attraction continuously to individuals regardless of gender. What we call the charisma of another person is nothing other than genuine attraction.

Pansexuality [B]

Martinello, 6:30 PM on another day

In our group recently entered two men, friends of one of our friends, Sfridonio and Pourtasio. They are very nice and make me laugh a lot. I even got close to one of them with whom I used to go running, and it was precisely while talking to him in the morning that I found out that... they are boyfriends! Since then, I started observing them more closely and noticing things I hadn't noticed before. No, certainly no prejudice there, quite the opposite. The issue is definitely not that they are a couple, absolutely not. There's nothing wrong with it, in fact, I have always been a supporter of freedom in love, but I admit I feel a certain embarrassment when they are together. Not when we are all together in the group chatting, joking, laughing, having a drink, but when they hug each other, hold hands. They've started kissing in the past few days as well. And then there's an issue... not a serious one, but there is. Sometimes I bring my son with me, maybe because I don't have time to take him home before our evening plans. Then he asks me a lot of questions, and I start to worry that this might disturb his natural sexual development. I wouldn't want him to think that it's normal for the world to go, how should I put it, in that direction. I know that attraction is innate, but maybe behaviors different from the norm could disturb him. I know it's not like that, I've always said so, but I... I just don't know what to do. A classic in the erotic dreams of us men is to imagine two lesbians exchanging all sorts of effusions, even making love! I imagine myself there, close to them. Yes, I know that if they were lesbians, I wouldn't care much about them, but I go crazy at the mere idea of seeing them together. But yes, I indulge in porn where there are lesbian couples, of course, I can't deny it. But two men...

75 Champion of gender ^A

Romolo, 1:40 PM on any given day

This whole issue of gender discrimination has tired me out. Women and men are equals! Everyone, regardless of gender, can do even the toughest and most difficult jobs if properly trained. A trained woman can knock me out with half a punch if she wants, just like a man. And similarly, an untrained man can be easily brushed aside by anyone who is even slightly trained, regardless of gender. This whole thing about household chores is purely cultural, but it's time to overcome this absurd barrier of gender-related tasks. Can you believe it? Men who don't wash anything at home, who don't change diapers, who don't iron, and claim to be cooperative just because they interrupt their couch activities, read compulsive channel surfing, to fix an electrical outlet that has come off the wall, an event that occurs only slightly more frequently than the passage of Halley's Comet. Tables are set because women do it, houses are clean because women take care of them. But today, women work just like men, so this makes no sense anymore! And have you ever thought about expressions such as "the cleaning lady", "the caregiver", "the secretary", etc.? No one hires "a male cleaner" for their home. It's also assumed that a man won't measure up because in the end, they engage in such tasks so rarely that it's highly unlikely they would be skilled at them. And TV? Shall we talk about that? Only a few bolder brands have made advertisements showing men doing household chores. For the rest, it's always and only women sniffing freshly washed laundry, using hyper-technological cloths for the floor. Oh, are we in the Stone Age? Speaking as a male... men, please, wake up!

Champion of gender [B]

Romolo, 6:20 PM on another day

I'm a very collaborative man, but I have to admit I struggle with changing my son's diaper and cleaning his bottom. It's not for lack of willingness, but honestly, I get a bit confused! I've also tried ironing, but with poor results. Every garment that survives the iron seems to come out more wrinkled than before! I spend an hour ironing a shirt and in the end, it's more creased than when I started. It's not that I'm sexist, but I think women have special abilities. And cooking? I tackle big dishes like the Sunday feast that I can prepare well, but during the week, my wife does the cooking. She also takes care of cleaning the bathrooms and kitchen, but mainly because often when I come home, I have to work to earn a little more. I do it for the good of the family! I'd like to be more helpful, but I don't always succeed. In the end, she's good at doing many things at once, and watching her, I've realized that the myth that women can do a hundred things while men can only do one is not just a myth. I know I shouldn't use sexist language, but sometimes it seems like they have a special talent, a superior sensitivity to cleanliness and caregiving, things that often elude us men. I'm certainly not a supporter of the patriarchal society, but if I try to do the things she does, I just mess up. Still, I pitch in: taking out the trash and bulky items, filling the water heater, and fixing a leaky faucet myself or calling the plumber. In short, I pitch in at home. No gender stereotypes here!

76 Sexual freedom - II [A]

Mariellino, 2:30 PM on any given day

Today's news is that the principal of an Italian school has entered into a romantic relationship with one of her students! Are we crazy? Sure, the student was of legal age and the law permits it, but it's still unacceptable! Come on! You're his teacher, the one who should be guiding him, teaching him how to navigate the adult world, even giving him tips on handling relationships! You should care for him, not sleep with him! In just a few moments, the social universe, and media in general, have been flooded with harsh judgments against the woman who has been rapidly socially labeled. But rightly so, I say! And then, I dare not imagine her situation with her own family, with the boy's family, with her other colleagues! Perhaps the most embarrassing thing for her, as highlighted by a speaker on one of my favorite radio shows, is that her own young students were the first to expose her to public ridicule. It should be noted that these same students had protested in the streets against another teacher a few months ago, who had allegedly called her own student a 'prostitute' for dancing on desks with her belly button exposed. Yes, perhaps it's not very consistent that now the students call the teacher a 'prostitute', but I understand them! Let's return to the principal... no one has shied away from judging her in the worst possible way, and I haven't either. Okay, fine, I'm the first to not get upset about anything anymore, but we entrust our children to schools and especially to all those who work there. It's not logical to think that schools themselves could create a psychological drama for our children with a relationship as truly borderline as this one!

Sexual freedom - II [B]

Mariellino, 9:30 PM on just another day

Today I went out with my longtime buddies from wild nights, Euterio, Frigenio, and Loperto. We often meet up during the year to share some beers and a good burger sitting at a table in some disco pub. Nothing particularly extraordinary, you know: we drink, we eat, and then we dance a bit to the DJ's music. Well, today the place started filling up after 11 PM, maybe thanks to the DJ's fairly well-known name. Groups of young adults started coming in, and even some groups of girls, all of legal age... simply stunning! Ah, the blessed youth. Wow. Too beautiful! You can tell they're naturally beautiful, but all dressed up for the evening, they shine like stars! Oh, the pain... my friends and I start making comments about them, at first quietly, then more openly. I feel a bit embarrassed because one of my friends, Frigenio, has a daughter around that age. I would never want him to think I'm some guy ogling such young girls. But it's pretty clear he's also into the comments and appreciates the presence of these beauties a lot. Oh my... they're so beautiful that if a judge accused me of having impure thoughts, I'd suggest they look at them first before passing judgment on me. Euterio and Frigenio suggest we try dancing near them and who knows... Loperto refuses, denying his availability, saying they could be our daughters, and Euterio responds that technically they could be, age-wise, but they're not. He adds that love knows no age. We all laugh and head towards the dance floor. Thankfully, the girls are there alone, otherwise we might risk a brawl. I fancy one of them, but I know I'm too old for her. But damn, she's so sexy...

77 Love and betrayal [A]

Ettorina, 6:00 AM on any given day

Love is serious business! If two people love each other, that relationship is sacred and should be defended at all costs. If true love lasts for many years, there must be a reason for it! When love is born, it's like igniting a fire that burns fast at first, then slower, but it still burns. Of course, things change somewhat after many years, but love remains. Life has its ups and downs, that's well known, and we all deal with this continuous ebb and flow! Fidelity is a value, and I don't understand how betrayals and separations can happen. I have morals, and I know perfectly well that certain things will never happen to me. Those are things for weak people with flimsy morals. The person I love is inseparably bound to me as I am to them, and that doesn't change just because an attractive person passes by. Many times I've been in situations where people liked me a lot and I didn't mind them either, but I've always kept it to a quick chat, at most a coffee at a bar, and nothing more. I am careful not to accept invitations for external meetings. There would be nothing wrong with it for me, but accepting would still signal availability to the other person, and I simply am not available. Plus, I would never want to give rise to gossip from anyone who might see us at a bar or wherever. My partner wouldn't take it well, despite trusting me. Sure, I could tell them without problems, but even that would be difficult for me. Saying, 'I'm going to have coffee with this person at such and such time', would unnecessarily cause fear, a thousand questions, doubts, and fears about the reasons for such a meeting. And I don't want to cause unnecessary pain to the person I love!

Love and betrayal [B]

Ettorina, 6:00 PM on another ordinary day

At the school where I work, there's a teacher who is truly very well-prepared. He's also a very attractive man, but that matters little except for the countless admirers who pursue him. In school board meetings, we often find ourselves as allies. This is because we always agree, which is both rare and pleasant. We've had coffee together several times, and I must say I feel really good when we talk. Some time has passed now, and after many coffees and pleasant moments spent in complete naturalness, especially amidst enjoyable laughter, we've decided to have a drink together after work. After all, what harm is there? My psychologist says I'm viewing this friendship as an escape from everyday life problems. Yes, she's right. I've been having several issues at home, and this new development, this moment of serenity, I admit, represents a breath of fresh air in my suffocating life filled with arguments and problems. Even my colleague isn't going through a good time, but he didn't want to talk about it, and I didn't press. I don't want to be burdensome or pushy; I prefer to be light and pleasant. I want to be for him what he is for me, that's all. In the end, we're not doing anything wrong; we're simply giving ourselves a break to refresh. Through this person, I've discovered that life can still be enjoyable. Each of us should seek happiness, right? So why should I live only in suffering? Well, things progressed a bit, and now we have a relationship. But it was normal given the point of no return my husband and I had reached. Too many arguments marked our days. Anyone in my place would have done the same. It's easy to say 'that would never happen to me'. My story isn't like others... mine is different, and he is special!

78 Swinging ^A

Fritullo, 9:35 AM on any given day

I often read news that leaves me quite perplexed, to which I'm not accustomed at all, perhaps due to my Christian-Catholic upbringing or because they truly seem absurd, I don't know. But either I'm a troglodyte puritan or we're at the limits of decency! Let's talk about this phenomenon of swinging. Couples of strangers, who have never met before, perfect strangers exchanging partners to spend steamy nights with. I don't want to be prudish, but it's immoral, it undermines the sanctity of the couple, the bond between two people. Many of them are even married! I mean... am I supposed to approve of my wife having sex with someone else whose wife or partner is having sex with me? But come on, what happens to their bond? Doesn't the institution of marriage mean anything to them? And how can they watch their own partner in a physical love relationship with a stranger and even claim to feel excitement? Is it possible that no jealousy arises in their hearts? Is it possible that no moral qualm affects them? I find this way of behaving completely absurd. It's certainly a product of these crazy times. I don't want to sound old-fashioned, but maybe in my father's time, none of this would have happened. Yes, I've read that despite swinging being punished by the law, it has been practiced since ancient Greece and ancient Rome. So what does that mean? It simply means that perverse people have always existed and unfortunately, always will, regardless of time and place. Yet this practice is becoming more and more widespread, and the motivation often seems to be a couple's desire to reignite the passion that fades due to the long time spent together. Seriously, at this point, why not work on that together? What's the point of adding external factors? Hmm, I really don't know...

Swinging [B]

Fritullo, 2:35 PM on another ordinary day

I have a beautiful relationship with my partner, but lately, nothing really exciting has been happening between us, especially from a sexual perspective. It's true that we still kiss sometimes, which shows there is passion, but perhaps it needs to be awakened a bit. Unfortunately, unlike before when both of us were clearly engaged, she sometimes seems almost annoyed now. This saddens me because I have a strong desire for her, but I feel somewhat embarrassed. I certainly don't want to be 'tolerated' but rather 'desired'. It has become embarrassing to talk about these issues. If someone doesn't want you, talking won't change things. This decline is mortifying me, and I'm constantly disappointed by how things are going between us. Well, we're all human! I don't consider it cheating, but I must confess that when the opportunity arises, I don't mind having an adventure with someone available. Even sparks can fly between neighbors. Infidelity? Absolutely not. These are just small escapes, outlets for stress and boredom that ultimately can even strengthen the main relationship without harming it at all. Since I've had these small freedoms, I've been much happier with her because the main problem is no longer there. In fact, I believe she does the same, but like me, she would never admit it. However, I'm not naive, so if she does it, why shouldn't I? No, there's no jealousy towards her, and why should there be? In the end, it's something that stabilizes our relationship, providing stimuli that were otherwise lost, so ultimately, we're better off now than when we were faithful. Love is love, and it's something that transcends pure and simple sex aimed solely at individual pleasure. It seems so obvious to me...

79 Hot videos and sexism [A]

Samuele, 12:00 PM on any given day

I learned, watching various news reports on TV and then several posts on social media, that a very young girl tragically committed suicide after her incredibly foolish and reckless ex-boyfriend, as an act of revenge porn, spread several videos of them together in intimate moments among their common friends. It's terrible that things like this happen. Not being able to accept the end of a love story and seeking revenge by destroying the life of someone you once loved, or at least claimed to love. It's sad to say, but nowadays it's extremely dangerous to record videos when you're intimate with someone, not because of the act itself, which is actually very intriguing, I admit, but because of the possible consequences if the relationship ends, exactly like in this case. When you're in love, you have infinite trust in the other person. It's terrible that he, just because she didn't want to resume their relationship and started seeing someone else, would exact this petty revenge. But it's especially terrible that their friends, fully aware of how uncontrollable video content can spread on the web, didn't hesitate for a moment to share that material with others. Her ex boyfriend is certainly guilty, but then there are their friends, who are guilty too! They are the ones who, despite not being involved and not having a real motive (no matter how absurd the ex boyfriend motive was), shared the video knowing full well that no one would ever be able to control it again. A video or a photo on the web remains there forever. Once spread, there will never be any way to block it. Even if the Cyber Police tries to prevent further dissemination, there's no real way to stop it. It's all absurd, but it happened. And now that family mourns the painful premature death of their daughter. It's a tragedy!

Hot videos and sexism [B]

Samuele, 5:00 PM on another ordinary day

My colleague Venus is having an affair with my friend Hephaestus, unbeknownst to her husband, wife, and children! Hephaestus tells me that when they're alone, they do really crazy things, stuff like from an extreme movie! I'm not interested, but he loves to boast about these erotic exploits. We colleagues don't consider ourselves prudish or puritanical, but I must admit some of his stories seem quite improbable for our beautiful colleague who always appears proper, tidy, polite, respectful, almost constantly embarrassed at the office. Hephaestus claims she transforms in bed. We don't believe him and we told him so. And what did he do? Without her knowledge, he recorded a video with a hidden camera and then shared the file with us on chat, of course asking for utmost discretion. We watched it and... oh my, the guy was right, Venus really lets loose! I would have never imagined! Ouch, I'm just a guy and... watching that, well, wow. Hephaestus asked us not to share the video with anyone, so at the moment it's just us six, the closest colleagues, who have seen it. We're a team, we trust each other absolutely. What we promise, we keep. But then again, thinking about it, even my colleague Mars, who was once Venus's boyfriend, would keep the secret. Almost tempted... but yeah, let's keep this among us. We are responsible people and no one will harm anyone. By the way, I chuckle thinking about his face when he finds out how Venus transformed after they broke up, especially since he often complained about her reserve. I shared the video with him. Mars is a dear friend, someone I trust implicitly; if I tell him not to share it with anyone else, he surely won't, not even with his best friend and partner in a thousand adventures, Cidoimo!

Gamification 8/10

Paragraph	Only A OR B	Both A AND B
74 Pansexuality	☐ 0 points	☐ 1 point
75 Champion of gender	☐ 0 points	☐ 1 point
76 Sexual freedom - II	☐ 0 points	☐ 1 point
77 Love and betrayal	☐ 0 points	☐ 1 point
78 Swinging	☐ 0 points	☐ 1 point
79 Hot videos and sexism	☐ 0 points	☐ 1 point
TOTAL		

Peoples and cultures

When you travel, remember that a foreign country is not created to make you comfortable, but to make its own people comfortable.

Clifton Paul Fadiman

80 Clothing and the individual [A]

Mirella, 10:15 AM on any given day

I don't believe that clothes make the monk. How can one decide if a person is good or bad, poor or rich, sweet or severe based on what they wear? Clothes, accessories... we're talking about fabric, leather, or other materials that simply cover our bodies. Firstly, because public nudity is not accepted, at least in my part of the world, and also to protect ourselves from cold and heat. So, despite the importance given nowadays to fashion, to style, what everyone wears is just that: materials that cover the body. Despite the vast array of choices available, fundamentally, they serve no other purpose than this. Of course, clothes can be used to denote belonging, for example to a team, an army, the medical profession, a company, or a political party. In these cases, clothing can indicate an individual's role in society. I have nothing against how others dress outside of myself; surely one cannot judge someone solely based on what they wear. If a king wore a torn, yellow dress instead of his ceremonial robes, would he be any less a king? Absolutely not. And why? Because he is king for reasons infinitely more important than the clothes he wears. I don't disdain how others around me and those from other peoples and cultures dress. Everyone dresses as they want! Who am I to decide if a person is good or bad, normal or crazy, sexually defined or not, based solely on the clothes they wear? Everyone dresses as they see fit. What harm can a person who dresses in a very colorful manner or with particularly short or long clothes do to me? If a man dresses in a universally considered feminine way and a woman in a universally considered particularly masculine way?

Clothing and the individual [B]

Mirella, 5:15 PM on another ordinary day

Today, on the street, I saw some Indians, or at least I thought they were, in ceremonial attire. I was left speechless! I would say, without exaggerating, they seemed out of place. They wore brightly colored clothes adorned with all sorts of trinkets, buckles, buttons, and super colorful, sparkling shoes. I looked around thinking I was in a movie. It was too strange to see them there, in the city center, just steps from my office, dressed that way. They walked seriously and solemnly, without blinking, a sign that the ceremony they were participating in must have been important, at least to them. Hmm, I wonder how they can go around the city dressed like that! And don't get me started on African women wandering our beaches in their long, colorful dresses, absurdly carrying their poor children tightly wrapped in those cloth slings on their backs. Someone pointed out to me that our 'Western' brides look like very flashy gift packages, living favors with a thousand ribbons and veils. Okay, but what's the point? That's attire for one of the most important days of their lives, not something worn every day! Others tell me that even men in our latitudes dress strangely! What would be strange? Formal attire? Like simple, dark vertical trousers, a precise jacket, and a tie, or a hanging piece of fabric around the neck? What's so strange about that? It's attire meant to show respect for the people you'll meet, especially in professional settings or at particularly important events. You can't exactly go to a business meeting in shorts and a t-shirt, right? Or show up for an interview wearing brightly colored Hawaiian shirts and purple hair. How absurd. There are clothes that must necessarily be worn in certain situations, that seems obvious to me!

81 Habitual nationalism [A]

Savino, 6:00 PM on any given day

I'm fed up with these same four streets where I was born, grew up, lived, and still live. Goodness, it feels like forever that I've been seeing and hanging out with the same people, almost without interruption. I'm serious, the exact same people from nursery school, through elementary and middle school, to high school and university. And then, the same streets, the same shops, the same places, never anything new. I would really love to change that, to experience new and fascinating realities, different ways of living. I'm very interested in traveling abroad, too, to get to know what I don't know – places, people, customs. I believe that staying in the same place all your life severely limits your ability to broaden your horizons about the world. Unfortunately, I've only just realized this now. But it's not too late, I hope. When I think about it, we're all somewhat limited in this regard. You know that psychological phenomenon where if you grew up with a particular type of music and loved it deeply, you struggle to open up to new styles or new musicians? It's called 'musical paralysis', it sets in around the age of 30, and it pretty much affects all music consumers – streaming platform surveys completely confirm this phenomenon. Well, I believe the same happens with the places you live. After a certain age, you become less interested in traveling, meeting new places, new people, new customs. But unfortunately, this is extremely limiting. It confines us to a kind of provincialism that can last until death. The problem is that we risk thinking permanently that our present is the center of the universe! But that's not true, the world is vast and diverse, and getting to know it better should definitely be a wonderful experience!

Habitual nationalism [B]

Savino, 12:00 PM on another ordinary day

We visited various places this year, both near and far. We went north, to the cold, and I sorely missed the mild temperatures of my country. You can't imagine how much I cursed finding myself walking the streets at 20 degrees below zero! Damn it, how can anyone live like this? There's nothing to be done, the climate where I live is the best in the world. Then I traveled east. Everything was very beautiful, no doubt, but... the food?! I wonder how people can eat dishes like those and even call them specialties! Liquid stuff, acidic, tons of rice seasoned with every ingredient the human mind can conceive, often inedible! I struggled to find something edible. Want to compare it with a dish from my country? Even our worst restaurant would cook it in a way that would put all Eastern restaurants to shame. I searched for an authentic restaurant from my country, but nothing, just shameless imitations, as evident from the menu full of grammatical errors. There's another thing that negatively surprised me, and it's the attire of the locals. Seeing women dressed like that, men in tunics, well, it was really embarrassing. I looked at them with a mixture of pity and condescension, feeling perfectly at ease in my fantastic jeans and simple, practical t-shirt. The fashion of my country is unbeatable, we're the best on the planet, everyone knows it, it's a well-known fact. And then many other things, the absurd public transport, the boats, the houses, completely different, the internet connection missing in some places and everywhere in others. The complete absence of technology in some countries and the excess in others. You can't imagine how much I missed my country. It's the most beautiful in the world. Other countries are interesting, but never like mine!

82 Society and racism [A]

Nada, 11:15 AM on any given day

I am not racist! Not in the slightest way, and if anyone thinks otherwise, I would very much like to be proven wrong! Humans are all equal; physical characteristics are non-essential details. Skin, in its various colors, is just one of many features that visually define our bodies, but above all, they make us distinguishable from one another. I can differentiate Evaristo from Frigerio because the former has red hair, the latter has large ears; the former is very tall, the latter is average; the former has round eyes, the latter almond-shaped. And I already have a general idea of what their internal organs are like! The external physical characteristics of various human groups around the world stem from numerous factors: thousands of years of adaptation to the environment, climate adaptation at specific latitudes, and the places where these populations have lived, etc. However, these physical differences do not determine people's quality, behaviors, or psychology. None of this has any scientific basis. Furthermore, humans have always traveled, moving from one continent to another and mixing genes from various groups in an entropic manner. Therefore, unless we discover in some solitary valley a people who, from the appearance of the first individual to today, have never crossed the boundaries of their living space, none of us can belong to a 'race'. If we try to use this kind of comparison with the animal world, we can affirm that we are all so hybridized that we are essentially the same, except for minor details. There are no differences of any kind between people with different skin colors, just as there are none between individuals with different hair colors. These differences exist only in the minds of those who assert them!

Society and racism [B]

Nada, 11:15 AM on another ordinary day

I'm not racist, but I admit I feel uncomfortable around black men waiting outside the supermarket! Every time I finish shopping and leave my market, there's always a young man with dark skin offering to carry my grocery bags to the car in exchange for a tip, or help me load the trunk, or simply return the empty cart while asking for the coin inserted. Of course, they don't harm anyone; in fact, they help me and even give me some nice compliments. Unfortunately, it's clear they are finding ways to get by, and this 'activity' helps them make ends meet. I've encountered several of them inside the supermarket who seemed to be shopping normally. Perhaps the management of this supermarket provides them with groceries for essential items. A really kind gesture! Recently, I was in London for work. I was staying at a top-notch 5-star hotel on the Thames, just a stone's throw from Big Ben. One morning, I went to the reception to request an invoice, and a young man of clearly African origin approached me to ask what I needed. Certain he couldn't assist me, I asked him to get his manager. He smiled and told me he was the Hotel Director. What a moment... I was astonished and embarrassed for several seconds, and I apologized dozens of times. It wasn't racism; there was no prejudice in my request. Perhaps I discounted the possibility that someone of color could hold such a role in my country. Upon returning, I shared this with my friends, who accused me of prejudice. The truth is, that gentleman is one of the few who studied and worked to attain such a prestigious position. I didn't expect it and made this gross error in judgment. I challenge anyone!

83 Society and migrants - II ^A

Sebastiano, 12:30 PM on any given day

Do migrants steal jobs? Those who claim this don't understand where they come from. A country on their continent, where extreme poverty is rampant, appears on paper as the 4th richest country in the world in terms of natural resources: copper, cobalt, coltan, diamonds, gold, zinc, uranium, tin, silver, coal, manganese, tungsten, cadmium, oil! Nearly all the cobalt used in batteries worldwide comes from there! Resources that make the rest of the planet drool and represent a 'death sentence' for many of its 84 million inhabitants. For these resources, the West allows various local tribes to clash so the country remains in constant war, always in debt. These riches alone could feed the entire Europe with its 740 million inhabitants for hundreds of years! So why is there poverty? Because children work in these mines, digging with bare hands even for uranium and dying? Falling into mining shafts and never coming out? If they manage, they sell everything to many multinational corporations in exchange for crumbs of bread? It's simple... Because we need the newest model of smartphone with the ultra-shiny screen! The map of companies in that continent is full of flags of Western multinationals that effectively extinguish any sparks of local entrepreneurship. We make them dependent and then say if they haven't developed, it's their problem! And if, in desperation, they cross their enormous continent on foot, get thrown into terrible cells, cross the sea on a dinghy with 200 others (I'd crap myself on a pedal boat), and try to reach our shores, dying, we say they deserve it, a good meal for the fish. If they don't die, we immediately think they're here to steal our jobs! Jobs that we would never do!

Society and migrants - II [B]

Sebastiano, 12:30 PM on another ordinary day

I would never do a humble job. In theory, all jobs have the same dignity, from the hyper-director to the porter. However, I don't think I would ever work as a porter or a laborer. But not everyone has studied like me and made a brilliant career climbing the ranks of my construction company to the point of reaching the top and actually being in charge. It's nice to be in this position, even though it exposes me to many management and economic problems, as well as difficulties in finding human resources. Is it possible that no one wants to work on the construction site? There's so much talk about poverty and lack of jobs, yet I can't find 4 workers willing to work with a bucket and trowel. But my construction site needs to move forward and the building must be completed within the established deadlines. I sent one of my guys to talk to some young men from the continent across from us. They live by expedients, unfortunately for them, and don't even have the right to unemployment benefits because they don't have residence permits. I can't do anything about it (and neither can they) if the bureaucratic algorithms of the police stations are so inefficient. Generally, I'm someone who gets indignant if labor laws are violated, but what else can I do? I watch on TV the illicit activities committed by my fellow citizens and I'm disgusted. Yes, because there are fellow citizens who exploit other human beings, like them and like me, to fill their wallets beyond any reasonable sense. I just want to give them a piece of bread to survive and some money to send home. I can't regularize their status, but this will benefit their pockets. I certainly can't insure them, but what's the worst that could happen on my construction sites? I'm in a tough spot. This way, I can solve the problem while also doing something good for them, helping them get by!

84 Crossing the sea ^A

Pamela, 6:00 AM on any given day

It's incomprehensible, unnatural, that there are people who risk their own lives and those of their children to cross nations and seas just to reach other countries where they hope for a social and economic rebirth. I can barely understand those who truly flee from wars, violence, death threats, or other dangers. I say 'barely' because the way these escapes happen is still insane. Does it seem rational to you that a man, a father, but especially a woman and mother, would decide to cross a vast stretch of sea on a small boat, with a high likelihood of encountering storms, holding a newborn baby in their arms, with numerous helpless brothers and sisters in tow? Even in the most dangerous situation, I would never risk the lives of my little ones. Just the thought that a slightly higher wave could sweep them away, forever lost in the grey waters, terrifies me. I feel like crying when I think about how many times this has already happened. But the cause cannot be solely war, hunger, or even simply the search for better living conditions. These people are not normal; they have a strange, debatable bond with their children. I'm not even sure they truly love them, at least not like we love ours! I don't believe that a sane parent would ever endanger the life of their own child, flesh of their flesh, in such a reckless manner! Can you imagine? A boat, if you can call it that, barely able to stay afloat, filled with dozens, hundreds of people crammed even onto the edges? And you? Sitting on the edge because other desperate people certainly won't give up their spot for you, holding your child in your arms and praying the whole time. No, this is not humane. Surely, we are talking about people who love their children much, much less than we do.

Crossing the sea [B]

Pamela, 12:30 PM on another ordinary day

Those who live in the richest countries think that nothing terrible could ever happen to them. But in the end, the impossible happened. Armies of angry soldiers appeared where once there was a beautiful road with flowers on the sides. They said that everything that is ours belongs to them. They came to take back the land they believe we usurped. And so, they took us, beat us, arrested us. I was imprisoned for 2 months in my country, without knowing anything about my husband and my two older children, my elderly mother, my friends. And as they imprisoned me, they also told me they would kill them. We all screamed as they separated us, it was terrible. Maybe they are dead, I can't know. With my little one, I spent days of torment and terror in a room 1 meter by 1 meter where I didn't even have space to lie down. I made him lie down. Endless days thinking about my family, my loved ones killed for no reason. Months passed without eating, suffering from lack of water. Everything they gave us, I gave to my child to moisten his parched mouth. I drank my urine. They say that in our blood there is different blood from the so-called 'pure' blood of the original ethnic lineage. But how can it be determined exactly from whom I descend? And even if it could be done, how could I ever be guilty of this? I was born here, I have lived here, my whole life is here... And now I suddenly find myself being considered an unwelcome stranger. They released me from prison and forced me to leave with my child, otherwise they will finish us off, this time for real. I have to flee, now. They told me there is someone who can help us, but it costs a lot. I have hidden savings. But... where will my child and I go, where will we go?

85 Ethnic prejudice [A]

Teodoro, 1:30 PM on any given day

When an object is poorly made and of low quality, you can tell right away. Objects that break in your hands after only a few uses or even while you're still taking them out of their packaging. It's definitely cheap stuff! Come on, let's be honest, well-made, high-quality items don't break that easily. It's well known that cheap stuff is of poor quality and breaks easily. If we're talking about perfumes, detergents, even beverages, they're often toxic. If we're talking about toys, they're often dangerous for children. In short, whatever you buy, there's a high chance it's harmful. And it's absolutely not worth risking your health and that of others just to save a few cents. If I buy a pair of cheap scissors, I'll probably pay 2 euros. If I buy a good pair of scissors from a supermarket in my country, I'll pay 4.50 euros. But with the first pair, I'll probably end up in the emergency room, with the second pair, I won't. But then, what can we expect from a people who always eat only one type of food, boiled rice? They all work under the table, they're all the same and controlled by the regime. And the top of the top? They eat dogs! Can you believe it? A clearly domestic animal, eaten without mercy. And then they pollute and don't care at all, but there's only one planet! They don't know English, and that's a clear sign of their isolation from other civilizations. And then they copy, copy, copy everything, absolutely everything we Westerners create. They have practically built their economy on the backs of us... the originals. And they dominate the markets worldwide because they practice extremely low prices proportional to the quality of their products. We, for the same reason, are being overwhelmed! We definitely need to impose customs duties, block imports, defuse this bomb that could lead us to disaster.

Ethnic prejudice [B]

Teodoro, 6:00 PM on another ordinary day

I started a retail business for live music products. A wholesaler from Pina offered me an excellent product at a low cost, on which I could make a significant profit. I tested it in the test room. It is of good quality! I accepted. Some will say it's cheap stuff, but not everything that comes from that wonderful country is low quality. Let's not forget that 90% of quality everyday electronics are produced in Pina. I'm not just talking about the mouse, the keyboard, cheap stuff, but hardware from major Western manufacturers. The most prestigious brands produce in Pina precisely because the labor cost is lower and, even adding shipping costs, they can sell at a competitive price. From today, I also sell speakers with my brand! There are no valid and affordable white-label products in Europe, too many costs, expenses, taxes. I requested a quote in Pina, providing my own design. They made me an amazing offer with unparalleled scalability for large quantities. I accepted! I insisted that the quality of my products remain the same, and it has. Their internal laws are obviously different from ours, but things have improved, and if you ask them for a product that needs to work well, they make it. They even reimbursed my travel expenses for signing the contract. Speaking of the custom of eating dogs, I recently had a friend of German origin as a guest. We cooked hare stew for him. We brought it to the table, and he almost fainted. He explained that for them, the hare is a domestic animal, like the dog is for us, and that for them, the idea of eating it is absolutely unnatural. Not that I care at all, we like hare, they are the ones who are strange. They don't know what they're missing. But then, who decides whether an animal is domestic or not?

86 Tragedies and relativity [A]

Regina, 2:30 PM on any given day

A few days ago, some billionaires and their children embarked on yet another journey to 3,800 meters below sea level. Their destination? What remains of the Critanic. The wreck of the unsinkable ship that, by sinking, perhaps began its eternal life. I understand those who, if they can afford it, decide to descend to those insane depths in those tiny submarines to see firsthand what remains of that legendary ship, which at some point in life has been on everyone's mind. Unfortunately, the submarine stopped communicating a few hours after the start of the long descent, and those people were lost without a trace. There are hundreds of trips of this kind, but this time it went wrong. And those billionaires, who had spent about 250k dollars each, all died, disintegrated in an instant. This, however, was understood only after an exhausting race to rescue them, hoping to find the submarine and all of them still alive. Thus, hundreds of civilian and military experts mobilized with their ships, submarines, robots, sonar, and probes to try to rescue those people, imagining them prisoners in an inert steel tomb at insane depths, with unbearable pressures and extreme temperatures. But they died, and the world came together around the families mourning their lost loved ones. The saddest part is that perhaps the bodies cannot even be recovered, because in such extreme conditions, assuming anything remains, it is practically impossible to retrieve something as fragile as a human body, moreover reduced to a tenth of its normal size due to the pressure. What an infinite tragedy, what immense pain. The Critanic... wealth... inevitability.

Tragedies and relativity ^B

Regina, 4:45 PM on another ordinary day

The news is reporting about yet another boat that departed from the nearby continent's coast, carrying almost 500 illegal migrants on board, including women, some of whom are pregnant, children, and men. The boat was spotted by some passengers on a plane flying over that stretch of sea. Is it possible that no lookout or hyper-technological radar from any of the surrounding countries detected this vessel? The passengers on the flight alerted the steward, who then reported to the captain, who sent the alert to the ground, and so on. As always, the blame game is unfolding. The navy of my country does not want to intervene because they consider it to be someone else's responsibility, due to the point where the boat is located, which is outside our territorial waters. This is the official reason. The real reason, which we all know but no one declares, is that we cannot spend millions of euros to save all the refugees on the planet! Other states must also do something for these poor people. And if someone gets carried away by emotion, by the sense of emergency, and rushes to rescue them immediately every time, other countries will never feel the need to fulfill the duties they are called to. Therefore, we must hold the line and wait for someone else to intervene. The navy of the coastal country from which they departed is not intervening for reasons I haven't even fully understood. Now the news has given an update, it seems that the boat has capsized and then sunk. The few survivors are clinging to some floating objects, and it is unknown how long they will be able to stay there. A new blame game is unfolding. In whose territorial waters did the incident occur? Who is responsible? About 500 people have died. Well, they chose to take those risks? Reckless, serves them right.

87 The term 'inclusion' [A]

Tobia, 7:15 PM on any given day

Every time someone talks about any social field historically not participated in by people of different skin colors or women, but in which they are now fully participating, the term 'inclusion' is used. I find this term senseless, at least in this context, and I am stunned to hear people use it so casually. While doing so, they are certain they are saying the right thing, of being inclusive. I hear phrases like: 'I am for the inclusion of all peoples and cultures. Inclusion means that different peoples, people of different ethnicities, people with their peculiarities, are included in all processes, activities, celebrations, and manifestations of modern society without any limitations'. Now... what sense does the term 'inclusion' make? Inclusion of what? Of what kind? Are we all equal or not? We really are, damn it, it is absolutely true that skin color, hair color, and other millions of details that distinguish one human being from another are equivalent! Okay, so what the hell does 'inclusion' mean? What does it mean to 'include' someone who already has the right to be included? Who do we need to 'include' who isn't already part of the single human race? It may seem like a terminological problem, but thinking about it, it denotes a much deeper-rooted issue. Few people realize that 'inclusion' is a completely wrong term. Now... I understand that coming from the deep past, from eras where inequality was ubiquitous, and living through a long transition like the one we've been in for about 800 years, it is necessary to undertake awareness campaigns, because statistically, this damn 'inclusion' still isn't there, but I believe that the solution is far from being found!

The term 'inclusion' [B]

Tobia, 9:45 AM on another ordinary day

Finally, my company has started hiring people of different ages, both younger and older, who have different skills and life stories, coming from various continents, of different genders, balancing the excess of male presence with a bit of meritocratic female representation. In short, it's a celebration of novelty in what was becoming a stifling environment. It's a real asset, something that can only make us grow. Getting to know new habits, cultures, languages, ways of thinking can only help us move away from provincialism and embrace a world that is much broader than the four streets around our home! Recently, some new executives have also been appointed, and heading my area are a man of South American origin for the operational side and an Asian woman for the organizational side. Our two new heads are, professionally, at least on paper, excellent. They have long resumes with countless experiences leading various company areas. On a personal level, they are pleasant but very quiet and do not like wasting time on frivolities. Well, the company is obviously not interested in the ability to socialize or empathize, but in professional qualities. Okay, it's clear, but I have some doubts about their ability to manage something as complex as the area I work in. Okay, the resume is impressive, but the complexity here is unlike anywhere else. And then, I don't want to be discriminatory, but a woman heading the organization, a woman, facing the countless brutal meetings that end with notebooks flying, I don't see it, I don't think she's suitable. As for the operational side, again, I don't want to be prejudiced, but... should a man from the siesta countries really lead our frantic operations?

Gamification 9/10

Paragraph	Only A OR B	Both A AND B
80 Clothing and the individual	☐ 0 points	☐ 1 point
81 Habitual nationalism	☐ 0 points	☐ 1 point
82 Society and racism	☐ 0 points	☐ 1 point
83 Society and migrants - II	☐ 0 points	☐ 1 point
84 Crossing the sea	☐ 0 points	☐ 1 point
85 Ethnic prejudice	☐ 0 points	☐ 1 point
86 Tragedies and relativity	☐ 0 points	☐ 1 point
87 The term 'inclusion'	☐ 0 points	☐ 1 point
TOTAL		

Your neighbor

'Neighbor' are all those who press upon the skin of our selfishness

Luigi Santucci

88 Ways of dressing ^A

Rosuccia, 1:45 PM on any given day

Even though I comfortably wear what I occasionally buy in stores, well... I hate fashion! I really do, from the bottom of my heart. It makes us all stereotyped, the same, standardized. Everyone with the same clothes, shoes, scarves, jackets, the same colors, the same models, the same styles, often repeated after a certain more or less long interval. And all suggested by industry professionals who decide, as one of my favorite bands mentioned in a historic song of theirs, what is cool to wear and what is not. Of course, it's up to us to follow these guidelines or not - what we should or shouldn't wear to keep up with fashion. Some say that fashion is actually a great convenience for us because it delegates to others the difficulty of choosing an outfit, a suitable look that is pleasant, comfortable, but above all socially appreciated in a given historical period, without seeming out of context, out of time, out of place. I understand these statements, but I literally don't care. If I feel like wearing something, I wear it even if it has been out of fashion for years. I do it because I want to, because it's easier for me, because I don't have to spend time and money buying new clothes every year and abandoning the old ones. I don't deny that I might like fashionable clothes, okay, it's possible, but ultimately this use and throw away, buy, wear, and discard, is too unsustainable for me, for my wallet, for society, for the planet. And finally, without being too much on the side of the hippies, I like originality. I like people who dress as they please, who don't have issues with it, who show their confidence even in their clothing. It's pointless to repeat it, clothes don't make the man; I can't judge someone just by how they dress.

Ways of dressing [B]

Rosuccia, 5:15 PM on another ordinary day

I'm on the metro in Paris, waiting for the train. At a certain point, a guy dressed in a strange way approaches. He's wearing black combat boots, ripped jeans decorated with chains and trinkets. He has about ten belts around his waist, all crisscrossed, which would take half an hour to open and close. On top, he's wearing a vertically striped brown and black shirt, not bad, maybe the only thing that's appreciable. He's adorned with dozens of necklaces and bracelets, clip-on earrings like those grandmothers wear, and to top it all off, he has a black beret with a decorated visor on his head. Through the rips in his jeans, you can see black lace women's tights. I don't understand... is he a man or a woman? He must be gay! But who is this? Where does he come from? Who dressed him like this and why? It's unsettling... With all those trinkets, he makes a lot of noise when he walks. Better that way, in case he has bad intentions, I'd have an advantage in running away. I don't want to be quick to judge, but he scares me a little. I hope he doesn't sit near me. I would never dress like that, at least not if I had good intentions, and for heaven's sake, surely he knows how different his outfit is from the standard. Okay, everyone can dress as they like and in full freedom, but in this case, you really can't consider it normal. I'm someone who accepts everything and everyone, but there's a limit, of course. How can you think of going around dressed like that without being considered strange, dangerous? In my opinion, he even scares children, and with his ambiguous appearance, he surely creates confusion in the minds of the kids here who look at him in bewilderment. What will they think? Is he male? Female? Young? Old? Okay, tolerance, but there's a limit to everything! The conductor is coming, I bet this guy doesn't have a ticket!

89 Discomforts and suffering [A]

Efesino, 4:35 PM on any given day

It is wonderful to support others, especially when they are going through a period of suffering. It is wonderful to be there when someone needs to be supported, helped, even just simply listened to. Stepping outside the limited perimeter of your own self and dedicating yourself to another, alleviating their suffering, putting yourself aside and offering support to their weaknesses... it is rewarding. It's truly a beautiful feeling! When you get the chance to do so, you feel really... good. Unfortunately, not everyone is able to be so altruistic, and just when you need to be consoled and talk about your problem to others, they, instead of appreciating your gesture and offering you a bit of their time to ease your moment of crisis, unload their own dramas on you. Recently, I went through a tough time, and as if by the book, one bad thing led to another to the point that it seemed like there was no end to the negative events. I had serious health problems, a massive financial shortfall, and I repeatedly risked losing my job. In those moments, I really needed someone who was willing to just spend some time with me to listen, that's all. An old friend called and asked how I was doing, I suggested we grab a coffee and he immediately agreed. We met, and he asked how things were going for me. I started to explain, and already after talking about my health, he said that my sufferings were nothing compared to his. And so it went on through work, money, family, and a thousand other areas of... suffering. I was so upset, seeing all my problems ridiculed, belittled! I was seeking support, help, I was hoping for a push to move forward, but instead, I found myself facing someone who told me that my problems didn't matter compared to his. What an absurd, total lack of empathy!

Discomforts and suffering [B]

Efesino, 6:15 PM on another ordinary day

Today I ran into my friend Paolino on the street. It was nice to see him again. I immediately asked him how he was doing, hoping for a smile and confirmation that life was treating him well. But no, he started off by saying that his taste buds were disrupted, his elbow was somehow connected to his foot, and that recently, after a domestic accident, a bruschetta had hit his eye. Because of these health issues, he is seeing several specialists. I don't want to downplay what he's saying, but... it seems to me like it's just a small elbow pain that won't go away, but is surely bearable. However, according to him, it hasn't healed despite the numerous, in my opinion useless, therapies he's undergone so far. If we were still close, I'd tell him to ignore these trivialities and go for a walk every day for half an hour. I think Paolino's problem is in his head, nothing like my health issues. Those cause indescribable suffering. Ten minutes have passed, and he's still talking only about his blessed knee... he has no shame, he has no idea what it means to be seriously ill and suffer severely. Enough! I interrupt him and tell him how I'm doing physically. That's it! He tries to go back to talking about his knee, but I press on with my problems, serious problems, and I prevail. He realizes that his are just quirks and nothing more. The cherry on top, he tells me about the mechanical issues his car is having, and I outdo him with the problems my car is facing. I understand that people need to be listened to, but there is an objective scale of severity, and his aren't real problems. Well, I think I did him a favor in the end; he'll have learned not to exaggerate and will understand that his troubles are truly insignificant compared to others'!

90 Social network - II ^A

Tessalonico, 8:38 AM on any given day

I'm not a big fan of social networks, although I have an account on practically each one of them. I'm registered everywhere, it's true, but I don't actively maintain my profiles and timelines like many do. I check what's happening here and there, and rarely post or share anything. However, I must admit I'm always amazed by the heated arguments over trivial matters that suddenly flare up, even among friends who have known each other for a lifetime and have always loved each other, at least until that moment, a moment that will forever change their story because then they will only want to suppress each other. I think social networks are a relatively new way to channel the anger that each of us accumulates during stressful days. Let's face it, we're all inflated like balloons full of resentment, so it only takes a little something, it could be a wrong word, a poorly written message, or an expression of an opinion contrary to ours, and... boom! We explode, uncontrollably dumping all our venom on someone who will react just as vigorously. And then there are the misunderstood messages, where someone meant to say something but, due to the wrong written formulation of thought, the wrong disposition of the reader's mood, the absence of facial expressions, intonation, and many other components that are present when face to face, they are misinterpreted and often cause irreparable damage to friendships that may have lasted for decades without any damage. As I've said before, I'm not interested in these pointless skirmishes, and in any case, no superficial discussion can compel me to come to blows with a friend. I'm out of these fights to the last blood on senseless topics.

Social network - II [B]

Tessalonico, 6:42 PM on another ordinary day

I read a post from a dear friend about the pandemic. It was senseless... he hypothesized a global conspiracy to kill part of the population. I don't even want to delve into the details of his posts, but what he wrote is delusional. Who can possibly manage a global conspiracy? Since when has there been a world government made up of people conspiring to exterminate us? But then the anger rises when I read phrases that point fingers at these imaginary conspirators with the term 'they'. 'They' decided, 'they' force us to do that, 'they' want us all dead... but who are they? Who, damn it? Enough, my anger is through the roof, now I'm going to give this absolute idiot a piece of my mind (and I even call him a great friend). I wish I had him in front of me to slap some sense into him for his utter idiocy. My goodness, I'm really feeling an uncontrollable urge to shut him down with words, for now that's it, but who knows what might happen one day. Who authorizes these people to write such things on social media? Don't they have a shred of intellect? We should activate a registration filter, if you're detached from reality and spew such nonsense, you shouldn't be allowed to complete registration. That way, with a simple questionnaire, we could solve the problem by preventing the spread of fake news like these. Freedom of speech? Yes, of course, who would question that I'm a staunch defender of everyone's freedom to express themselves and state their ideas, naturally, but there's a limit to everything! These aren't ideas, they're distilled idiocy. And they might influence other weak-minded individuals like themselves. Enough, I'll respond with a comment and tear him apart with words, explaining to him as bluntly as possible how absurd his statement is and how much damage he's causing!

91 My son-in-law ^A

Ubaldo, 1:30 PM on any given day

My beautiful, sweet, and unique daughter, Greobalda, has now grown up! From her first cry until today, it has been wonderful and challenging to follow her, because my daughter has always had a strong-willed character, which was evident right from the start. Then, when she reached adulthood, she naturally began making decisions independently, as it should be. So, she directed her studies in a direction that I didn't initially understand, but which turned out to be right for her. Greobalda has studied hard, always achieved excellent grades, and never gave me any reason to worry. Well, my wife and I are truly satisfied. She is about to graduate now, and then we'll see... work, family… these are all things that are hers now. As parents, we have completed our guiding journey, so to speak. Of course, we will always be there for her; the family bond is unbreakable, as you know. But after this important step, she can be considered independent. Do I have dreams for her? What father wouldn't have dreams for their children! For Greobalda, I dream of a job with an important role that doesn't prevent her, if she wants, from starting a family, because I also dream of becoming a grandfather and pampering some beautiful grandchildren. I would like her to create her family with a partner who proves to be, well, a good person. I'm not talking about someone with necessarily outstanding qualities, I simply want my daughter to be with someone who will love her as she deserves, who can continue the great love that we have for her, who respects her and is respected by her. No, no specific expectations other than this. I certainly cannot choose for her, that's clear, nor would I ever express my opinion on someone she introduces to me as her partner. But I can certainly allow myself to hope!

My son-in-law [B]

Ubaldo, 6:30 PM on another ordinary day

Greobalda will come by today to introduce us to her boyfriend, Ermenesippo. She told my wife Fruisina that she's head over heels in love with him. She speaks of him as a kind, helpful, gentle, supportive, and very cooperative man. We have high hopes, I admit, and we are both excited. Here they are! I hear my wife opening the door and greeting them. They enter the living room, where I am sitting on the couch pretending to read, feigning indifference, and they introduce him to me. I stand up, close the newspaper, and flash a smile, shaking his hand. Ermenesippo has such a strong grip! Compared to him, my hand felt like a cold cutlet left out for six days. He's wearing black jeans and a white t-shirt, and he's very tanned. He must be one of those lawyers who loves beautiful women (my daughter), beautiful cars, and the good life... sun, sea, boats, etc. After some small talk, I ask Ermenesippo what he does for a living. He says he works for a construction company on construction sites. And I say, "Ah... an engineer?" And he says, "No." "A surveyor?" And he says, "No." "Then what?" And he says, "Jack-of-all-trades laborer." I smile, but inside I think... What on earth? My daughter is with a jack-of-all-trades laborer? Just the term "laborer" to me means everything and nothing, and certainly means "low-level", compared to our social background, but "jack-of-all-trades"? So, he's so basic he doesn't even have a specific role? Like a mason, a tiler, I don't know... nothing. Okay, he's kind, he even speaks, strangely, good Italian, but my daughter deserves more, she deserves someone of higher social standing. He surely loves her, cares for her, but is it possible that a woman accomplished in life like her should settle for so little? As soon as they leave, I'll talk to her and try to reason with her! "Jack-of-all-trades laborer"... Really?

92 Kindness and public transportation - I [A]

Fulcilio, 2:00 PM on any given day

I'm on the subway that goes from the airport to the central station of my city. We all got off the same flight and there are many people with suitcases, children, backpacks. They are sweaty, tired, stressed, just like me. The train is crowded and there are no free seats. I stay standing at the end; I'm still young and strong, no problems, even though the train jostles us around quite a bit. At an intermediate stop, a very young woman gets on, loaded with bags, with 2 children in tow, one very small and one a bit older, cute and lively. She doesn't ask, but it's clear she deserves to sit down due to the difficult situation she's in, yet no one makes a move to offer their seat. I look around scanning all the comfortably seated people, mentally ruling out those who couldn't give up their seat due to age or the amount of luggage they're carrying. Not them, not them. Ah, there, that group of very young friends and those 2 young gentlemen. They could definitely give up their seats to the woman and her bags and children. But no one seems willing to do so. They've noticed the situation but pretend not to, turning slightly as if to simulate complete indifference. The woman, in distress, says nothing, asks for nothing, although she deserves it in some way, and with great dignity gazes wearily out of the window. Surely she hopes someone will offer her their seat, but nothing happens, absolutely nothing. I'm outraged, truly disappointed in human nature. I try to look the young people in the eyes, try to make them understand that someone needs support, that a small gesture could make a big difference to this family, but nothing at all. They remain completely indifferent, the group of young people and adults who could give up their seats stay in their unyielding indifference. I can't believe it... What kind of humanity is this?

Kindness and public transportation - I [B]

Fulcilio, 2:00 PM on another ordinary day

I've just returned from a long business trip. I caught the first flight today at 4 in the morning and now it's 5 PM! I'm about to board the bus that will take me home. I'm exhausted, my bags are heavy, I'm sweating like a mule; I can't take it anymore. I find a seat and pounce on it immediately like a javelin at the Olympics. Finally, I'm almost home and can relax a bit. The bus stops at the intersection of Ossimoro Street and several people get on, including a very elderly woman, so old that in her age, which I'm not young myself, I'd fit in almost twice. She has difficulty walking, leaning on any available support, appearing very fragile. But no, not this time... I know kindness, empathy would dictate that I give up my seat, but there's a limit to everything. I'm really tired, I've worked so much and haven't had a moment's rest since this morning. I turn my head towards the street and rest my forehead on the window. The lady might think I didn't see her. Come on, what's the big deal after all? If she's here, it means she's used to taking public transport, she's not as fragile as she initially seemed. Surely she's still strong enough to go grocery shopping or visit her grandchildren on her own. No, I can't move from here, I really want to stay. Okay, next time I'll give up my seat, but this time I'm at my limit. Old age doesn't mean having an absolute right to everything. Even young people who work have the right to rest, to enjoy a peaceful journey like this, to relax after an exhausting day. But then... this woman must have a family, relatives. They should accompany her instead of leaving her alone roaming the city. It's absurd, it shows indifference and insensitivity! Where are we heading?

93 Kindness and public transportation - II [A]

Uberta, 7:30 AM on any given day

I'm on the subway in Rome, heading from home to the office. Today, I'm running a bit late. I live in the suburbs and I get up very early to catch the metro in the morning. When I arrive, the station is half empty. Here comes the train! The journey takes about 40 minutes and my stop is in the city center, where parking any private vehicle would be impossible. Fortunately, the public transportation works decently. We're almost at my stop. I gather my things, put on my jacket, stand up, and position myself by the exit door, holding onto one of the many handrails available. Artificial light starts to filter through the windows as the train enters the station, as always, packed with people. The metro stops, the doors open, and I prepare to get off. But I can't! People waiting outside to board the train, instead of waiting for everyone to exit the carriage, start filtering through those of us who are getting off, creating a complete paralysis, delaying our exit, bumping into us, pushing us. All just to secure a seat! I'm outraged; it's an unwritten rule perhaps, but you should always wait for all passengers already on the train to exit before boarding. There's no need to explain something as obvious as this. It's pure logic! Nonetheless, this madness always happens! And here I am, standing, trying to make my way through these frantic, rude individuals, trying to get off my train and get to work. Just a few moments of patience and allowing us to exit would have made everything easier, not only for us getting off but also, and especially, for those getting on. What kind of humanity is this?! I look dismayed at my fellow passengers, exchanging their sympathetic glances regarding this act of rudeness.

Kindness and public transportation - I [B]

Uberta, 5:00 PM on another ordinary day

It's 5 PM and I've just left the office. Today at 6 PM, I have an urgent appointment, a long-awaited medical visit that cannot be postponed. I reach the subway station in 4 minutes; the journey takes about 40 minutes, and my car is parked at the station near my neighborhood where the medical office is less than 10 minutes away. If traffic cooperates, I should make it, but it's cutting it close. With a bit of luck, I could arrive almost on time, or maybe just 5 minutes late, which would be acceptable. But everything must go smoothly from now on. I rush down the stairs and reach the platform where, unbelievably, my train is arriving... I'm lucky! I position myself in front of it as it slows down, packed with people, as usual. Many need to get off and many need to get on. But if I miss this train, I'll be at least half an hour late. The doors open, and the mass of people on the train starts to exit. Slowly, damn it, too slowly! Look at that person taking one small step at a time! And that one, moving as if walking on eggshells? I'm in a hurry, damn it, and you all, what the hell are you doing? People with empty and boring lives, without appointments, without goals. I'm getting quite annoyed. And here comes the kid with the scooter. Enough! I'm getting on. I push through them like a salmon swimming upstream, confident that I can do it. An elbow here, a nudge there, a support there, and I'm in, while my ears pick up the discontent behind me. Some shout that the rule says you should wait for those already on the train to exit. Yes, that's true, but not today, not here, not for me. Today, I'm damn in a hurry that no one around me has or can understand. So step back and let me through!

94 Infants and weaning [A]

Diana, 11:35 on any given day

When I see 3-year-old children still breastfeeding, I am astonished. Come on! When will you stop breastfeeding them? When will you cut the second umbilical cord that it's not up to the surgeon to cut? Children need to grow up, and in this, you parents are crucial, especially in allowing them to go through each developmental step they must, and I emphasize must, face. Breast milk is good and sweet for a newborn, comforting, a panacea, a medicine, a soothing remedy. It's truly medicinal, miraculous, but it should be confined to the early months. Then you need to let go! The mother needs to let go, she can't be enslaved by this, always forced to go out in clothes that allow her breast to be exposed, showing her nipples to the world; the child needs to let go, gaining confidence and trust and projecting themselves into a world that may be less protected, but abundant in wonders. So to all those mothers I see breastfeeding 40-year-old children, I say, enough! Free yourselves and free them from this slavery! It's outdated for your child to suckle your breast while standing, almost taller than you! But really, there's a limit to everything. And do we want to talk about 12-year-olds sleeping in their parents' bed? It's entirely the fault of parents who didn't know how to break this habit at the right time, so when the child grew up and started reasoning, this nighttime closeness protected them from insecurities and early fears, becoming then indispensable. Enough! Get your kids out of your beds, come on! You bought them a nice, colorful, functional and spacious crib, take them there to sleep! It's big enough for them to go camping alone and make conquests, and you still keep them in your bed?

Infants and weaning [B]

Diana, 16:05 on another given day

My little Giosafatte recently turned 3 years old. I still breastfeed him. Why do I do it? Well, for several reasons that concern both him and me. I don't think I'll have any more biological children; I'm quite old already, and I'm not even sure I want to go through all those phases again – however wonderful – that lead a woman from conception to birth and everything else. Breastfeeding your own child is ancestral, wonderful, and emotional. Every time you have him in your arms, it feels unreal to experience that emotion that so many women before you have lived and others after you will live. Since the day the first *homo sapiens sapiens* set foot on this planet, this emotion has pervaded breastfeeding moments. So for me, it's not easy to stop, considering I won't be able to do it again, won't be able to live this moment again. So why deprive myself of it so soon? Yes, it's true, I'm generally against it, but mine is a different case: when my little Giosy is upset, crying, hurt, or feeling unwell, drinking from the breast calms him, soothes him, reassures him. Believe me, the breast is a powerful tool capable of bringing calm to a baby in distress. I meet mothers who almost ridicule me when they find out I'm still breastfeeding, and they even rudely advise me to stop, almost calling me self-destructive. But they don't understand, or perhaps they no longer understand the pleasure of breastfeeding. Or maybe it's just fashionable to say that to other mothers, but deep down, each one of them probably misses those moments of wonder. Oh, I forgot... Giosafatte sleeps in our bed. Maybe my husband is a bit nervous about it, but how beautiful it is to have this tender and defenseless little body next to you that occasionally throws its arms around your neck!

95 Peace and war ^A

Ugo, 19:00 on any given day

War is a terrible thing... it's always a frightening reality, regardless of the century in which it occurs, but if it happens in our times, there is nothing more anachronistic and terrible. Can we grasp it? Two 'modern' states, one against the other! A sovereign state attacking another sovereign state. And this isn't 1938... it's happening today! Suddenly, everyone living in the invaded state finds themselves thrust into a world that seemed forgotten. Once again, there are bombs, explosions, massacres, shootings, torture, and every other horror inflicted upon soldiers, women, young men, the elderly... children. I am against all forms of war, and this situation makes me furious. Imagine if tomorrow our country were attacked by a neighboring country... and we had to seek shelter in makeshift bunkers at the sound of sirens... and our homes were destroyed by an air raid... and suddenly we had no place to sleep, to eat, to live. Absurd, isn't it? Yet this has truly happened to those living in the invaded lands; they have experienced exactly this. And they couldn't do anything about it. Well, I wish that all international politics would make a tremendous diplomatic effort to solve the problem, and if that isn't enough, I would want friendly countries, including ours, to provide defensive weapons to the invaded country! Why? Because allowing it to happen, being indifferent in situations like this, is extremely dangerous. We cannot let people die in this manner in today's world. We must support them, rush to their aid, help them defend themselves, repel the invaders, fend off every attack, every bombardment. They must resist and repulse the reckless warmongers to regain their freedom and rebuild their country. This is the most important goal for all of us.

Peace and war [B]

Ugo, 09:30 on another given day

The price of methane is about to increase drastically due to the war between Castrazia and Islavinia. Just like that, in no time it has already increased threefold compared to last year. We'll have household bills reaching 600 euros at best! And then gasoline will also go up, and a full tank will cost more than what one earns in a day's work. On top of that, electricity bills and diesel prices had already recently risen. All this because we decided to punish Castrazia for invading Islavinia with various economic sanction packages. I understand this, but we can't bear this perfect storm of price hikes. Yes, because while the war is ongoing, we continue to import primary resources from Castrazia! In my opinion, we could support Islavinia even without these sanctions that are backfiring on us. Why should we provoke the leader of Castrazia so much? We are a small country, not actively belligerent, we are, so to speak, on the defensive side, but then why economically attack such a huge country and provoke it, causing these understandable retaliations in trade? Okay, I admit it, war, deaths, civilian massacres, explosions, bombings, they're all horrible things and we definitely need to do something, but did we really have to take a hard stance on economic matters? There are many ways to show our support for invaded Islavinia, but this we simply cannot afford! I would be in favor of reversing course on the sanctions and returning to more moderate measures, so that the leader of the invading country can reconsider their decisions. Everything can be endured, but the cost of living is important for each one of us. And perhaps Castrazia has its own valid reasons, right?

96 Peace and revenge [A]

Serena, 08:45 on any given day

My outlook on life includes respect for others and human relationships. I believe that sincere dialogue is essential for building strong and lasting bonds. In my daily interactions, I always strive to practice these values, actively working to overcome any obstacles and conflicts. I believe that every moment of collaboration and mutual understanding is a small step towards a more peaceful and harmonious world. Long live peace, long live bonds, friendships, and good relationships! However, I am not someone who leans towards disputes or controversies. In every situation, both personally and professionally, I always seek to mediate and avoid unnecessary conflicts. I prefer to diffuse tensions and promote a climate of serenity and cooperation to maintain positive relationships with friends, family, and colleagues. I am convinced that petty arguments and insignificant conflicts are a waste of energy and a source of avoidable stress. That's why I prefer the path of non-belligerence, seeking to avoid confrontational situations and favoring open and respectful communication. In the workplace, I am inclined to find alternative solutions rather than engaging in heated confrontations. I prefer to seek common ground that satisfies both parties involved, promoting cooperation rather than anger and hatred. I firmly believe that educating towards peace and tolerance in everyday actions is crucial for building a society based on values of solidarity and mutual understanding. Every gesture of reconciliation and every effort to maintain harmony contributes to creating a better world, free from conflicts and divisions. Therefore, I join the chorus: down with war, down with quarrels, long live peace, long live bonds and friendships!

Peace and revenge [B]

Serena, 18:33 on another given day

We've just moved into a new house. I step into the communal garden for the first time, looking for a temporary spot to park and unload the boxes and bags I have with me. A man approaches, likely a neighbor wanting to welcome us. I get out of the car and smile, politely greeting him. He nods back and immediately chills me by asking to move my car and park somewhere else. According to him, leaving it there would make it difficult for one of his family members to maneuver. What? You don't even give me a welcome, and the first thing you say to establish good neighborly relations is this? If it were your own need, I might understand, but you're ruining our first meeting to avoid the risk that one of your relatives – who are guests here – might scratch their car in an unlucky reverse? But why should I care about your relatives' cars! Why should I care about you and your rude demands! I'm staying right here and no one will move me. Besides, it's right in front of my garage and I have every right to be here. No one ever parked here before me, and I will never, ever move my car from this space. You can pray to every saint you know, bother me every day, ask me endlessly. I will stay here until the end, and if you don't accept that, our relationship will be terrible. I will always be ready for discussion, reaction, banter, argument. Always inclined to start a debate, to reply sharply, to hit back with irony, sarcasm, and sharp remarks, but also, if necessary, to escalate things. And I will never forget how in just a few moments you destroyed what could have been a relationship, not friendship necessarily, but at least respect. Yes, because I am for peace, but if peace is denied due to pettiness, if it's not a value for you as well, then let there be war!

97 Bullying and cyberbullying [A]

Valterio, 13:45 on any given day

Bullying is a terrible social plague and should be eradicated as such. It's true that sensitivity regarding this issue has changed significantly in the last 30 years, so much so that what my peers and I considered minor pranks as boys would now be condemned as serious incidents. But there is true bullying, which is absolutely harmful. Children, teenagers who are subjected to bullying should be protected, supported, monitored, and the bullies should be seriously punished, not just verbally reprimanded. It's terrible that a young person can feel terribly alone, scared, fearing to leave school, to leave home, because they are afraid of encountering their... tormentors! Those who psychologically and physically abuse them, who make them a laughingstock in the eyes of others, who mock every vulnerability. And it's equally terrible that there are other young people who, without any reason, inflict this kind of gratuitous suffering on their peers. Often, a bullied child then becomes a bully in other contexts. Is it the fault of parents, of society? I don't know, but I can't imagine without horror that my own child could experience such episodes and become a victim of bullying. Something must be done. Parents must network with other parents and with schools to prevent these harmful actions by these children, unite against the occurrence of such episodes, be able to prevent them, understand the dynamics that occur among classmates, among friends, look beyond the surface and delve into the small changes in mood of our children to understand if there are psychological damages perhaps not clearly shown but hidden due to embarrassment. These incidents must absolutely not be minimized. Never again bullies!

Bullying and cyberbullying [B]

Valterio, 10:12 on another given day

The headmistress of the middle school my son attends called me. Initially, I thought she wanted to propose me as a candidate for the parents' representatives elections, but... no. She wants me to come to her office as soon as possible for communications of a certain importance. I asked her to give me some hints, but nothing. I immediately took time off work and went to see her. She told me something... absurd! It seems that my son has been accused of acts of bullying. But this is absolutely impossible! They must have made a mistake. My son is shy and a bit of a loser; he couldn't possibly be responsible for these despicable acts. Who could have spread these lies? The headmistress tells me that if it were just an allegation, she wouldn't have called me, but she has heard from several students and all point to my son as the main culprit in a series of bullying incidents. I am outraged; these are instigators, liars, probably envious of us and our status. My son would never behave badly towards anyone. She asks me to talk to him about it, and I tell her that I don't need to because I know my son perfectly (who better than me, after all?) and I am certain, absolutely certain, that he could not be the perpetrator of such acts. At most, if I really didn't want to call every child and parent a shameless liar, informers of such lies, I can imagine they confused a joke said in jest with a serious offense. And here is the malice of those who necessarily want to interpret something in a mean-spirited way, distorting its meaning with intolerable accusations. I am suing the headmistress, the school, the parents, and even the children for defamation! Liars, liars, and shameless!

98 Social network - III ^A

Silviana, 12:18 on any given day

I've been on social networks for many years and over time I've learned to understand them, managing my accounts well and using them in the best possible way. I like to post a few photos from time to time, share important moments of life. I enjoy telling something (briefly) about a nice or funny episode that happened to me, or an event I attended, like a show, concert, or event, but without exaggerating. Sometimes, when I feel like it, I open the app and read other people's posts, my friends' stories. I admit I often consider them... frivolous? Useless? But I appreciate the lightness they bring. Of the ways people use social media, I especially love that extraordinary self-irony that some remarkably intelligent people possess. And then... memes! How much I laugh seeing how they mock current myths. On the other hand, I don't like polarized discussions, where there are two opposing parties that, minutes after the post that generated them, unleash a guerrilla warfare in which positions become increasingly extreme and the debate... null. People who believe they can prove something, others who want to prove exactly the opposite, and no one really reads the content of each other's comments. It's all insults, completely ignoring the previous message. The other person doesn't agree with you? Insult them. The other person doesn't acknowledge your supreme knowledge of the subject derived from your renowned degree in 'everythingology'? You'd rather see them dead and can only try to channel the unbearable anger into the next vitriolic comment. But I'm not like that, I don't get caught up in those dynamics. I am a balanced and composed person.

Social network - III [B]

Silviana, 19:22 on another given day

I logged onto my favorite social media site to see what my friends were posting. I just read a comment that attributes a song to my favorite band, a song my favorite band never wrote. Guaranteed, for sure, I'm the ultimate expert. And I also know how this misunderstanding started! It's a fake news story that's been circulating since pre-Internet times. Many years ago, another band released this song, and it was mistakenly attributed to my favorite band. How this could happen, I have no idea, given that my band has a very different style and the singer's voice is much, much more baritonal than the other band's singer. But it happened. And now? I read a comment from a fan like me explaining what kind of misunderstanding this is. Well, I would have written it differently, citing authoritative sources, but it's fine anyway. I smile. But then I see that the author of the post is writing something. He's insinuating that my beloved band wrote that song and gave it to the other band! What kind of idiocy is this? Enough, I'm replying too, and this time, I'm citing sources. There, now they'll agree with me. What? They reply that I don't know anything about music and the history of music? How dare this charlatan? Me, who sang backup in several bands, who plays almost every musical instrument, who's been devouring music since I was three years old. But above all, me, who is a record collector of my band, one of the top experts. I can't tolerate this, I have to react and tell this xxxxx that it's better if he goes and xxxxx his xxxxx and that he can hang himself because he's just a xxxxx who doesn't even know how to wash his xxxxx. You are a xxxxx person, you make me sick, and you can only wallow in the mud like the animal you are. Really, if I meet you on the street, I'll kill you!

99 Women judging women [A]

Susanna, 10:30 on any given day

Sometimes I am amazed by the crude comments men make about us women. It happens especially when they judge someone who isn't present at the moment, like a new colleague, a colleague's partner, an ex-colleague, a friend, an acquaintance, basically any woman who isn't directly linked to them through a strong friendship or close family ties. And how do they talk about them? What do they judge? First, breasts and buttocks, then the way they dress. If the unlucky woman is young, attractive, and shapely, the comments are exclusively about physical appreciation, erotic desire, and declarations of possible sexual activities each of them would undertake with the person in question. If the woman is particularly beautiful and attractive, then at the first miniskirt, they unleash epithets that systematically associate her with the most famous prostitutes in the country. And above all, the decoding begins of the alleged reasons behind such attire… 'she wants to be the boss', 'she wants to hook up with this or that'… If we instead talk about someone overweight, not very attractive, not too beautiful, and who perhaps dresses in a less flashy, modern, or sophisticated way, then… all hell breaks loose… a barrage of insults, words of blame, denigrations, as if not being hot were a fault to be paid not only by feeling constantly devalued but also at a reputational level. All of this is terribly superficial, troglodytic, intolerable, and limiting. And then we talk about empowerment, equal rights, freedom… These losers are truly stuck in the Stone Age, they have prejudice dialed up to 3000 and a level of testosterone that in words sounds like that of an 18-year-old, but surely in action is more like someone in a nursing home. In short, mean and insensitive for no reason.

Women judging women [B]

Susanna, 12:26 on another given day

Today, a new colleague around 50 years old arrived at the office, although she looks more like 65 based on her skin and her face. She's dressed, according to me and my colleagues, in a way that isn't suitable for the context: a short, flowing light pastel dress, showing off her creased legs to everyone. Perhaps she overdid it with tanning in her youth, who knows. The ugly décolleté, clearly visible from the exaggerated neckline, highlights a sagging chest! How could she think to display it like that? I can understand a thirty-year-old with a firm, shapely chest, but a chest like that? And she shows it like that! And shall we talk about her behind? The colleague flaunts a low, droopy buttocks, even more saggy than her chest, one of those behinds that if men were to turn to look at it to assess it, they would be amazed after the first evaluation. She also wears heels, not extremely high, but high enough to further accentuate that behind. And then... her hair. What kind of hairstyle is that? One feels like asking her if she's attending a business meeting or a wedding! The makeup... heavy, bright lipstick and very dark eyeliner. Seriously, where does she think she's going dressed like that? Are we sure the new colleague knows she's been hired in a respectable company like ours, or does she think she's ended up in a brothel? Or worse, is she out to solicit? God forgive me for these thoughts, I know perfectly well that every woman is free to dress as she pleases, but when it's too much, it's too much! Even when we were twenty, we wouldn't have presented ourselves like that. Okay, freedom, empowerment, the possibility of not being judged superficially, but this surpasses every limit of decency. And her? She flaunts confidence, seemingly unaware of how she appears in the eyes of all of us. Bah, we're truly astounded.

100 Mediocrity on the track [A]

Brando, 13:18 on any given day

We have a company that allows aspiring drivers to live track driving experiences with supercars or race cars. We're talking about vehicles of every engine size and power. You can drive small cars, large cars, single-make championship cars, Gran Turismo cars, and even Formula cars. Not Formula 1, of course, that wouldn't be possible, but lower formula categories, yes. These are vehicles with tremendous power and capable of reaching high speeds, at least compared to street cars. We organize events on every track that permits it, all around the country, and our calendar is always full of bookings from users eager to challenge themselves with these truly special vehicles. The cost of these experiences is quite high and increases with the power of the vehicles used, but we're talking about a luxury that people indulge in once or twice in a lifetime, so the price is justified. Moreover, we are very skilled and accommodating in our profession. When a customer purchases a package from us, we immediately provide them with our contact number to arrange the experience via chat, starting from choosing dates and locations where we hold events, to driving tips. We strive to be friendly, kind, and above all, attentive to meeting their various needs. Our vehicles are not too difficult to drive, but you certainly shouldn't be afraid of finding yourself on a real track with a powerful machine in your hands, while others whose sole objective is to be faster on the next lap zoom past you, possibly brushing against you. But if this isn't a problem for our customers, then the experience will be truly exceptional. Maintaining our vehicles in top condition requires a lot of money, and we don't always manage to tune them perfectly, but if something goes wrong, we give our utmost and always act to protect the customer.

Mediocrity on the track [B]

Brando, 13:18 on another given day

It's Saturday and we're at a small track in the north for the Formula 4 event. We have with us our 2 Formula 4 cars, former stars from old Indian championships, still good enough to give our clients a thrill. It's been a while since we organized an F4 event, so the cars have service batteries that are dead, and there wasn't time to recharge them. On one of them, the alternator doesn't work, and since the battery drains faster than it charges, the car often stalls even when idle and with the engine revving. Buying new batteries and an alternator costs too much and we certainly don't want to cut into our profits! To work around this, before each client's turn, we install a fully charged battery that lasts long enough for them to complete their laps. The first two clients today had no issues. With a bit of luck, everything might go smoothly with the rest. Here we go, they're starting! Ouch, things aren't going well, the batteries are on their last legs. One car manages, but the other stalls even in second gear at full throttle. The client isn't at fault, poor thing, it's very difficult to drive like this. During a yellow flag, we reach him on the track and restart his car, admitting the problem to him. He's fairly understanding. The car restarts, but then the problem recurs two more times. In the end, the marshals force him to leave the track. He's angry and disappointed and demands a refund. Okay buddy, I understand your anger, but refunds aren't covered in the contract! Okay, the issue is caused by the vehicles, but you signed a document accepting everything without the possibility of recourse, and now you're crying about your money! Maybe we didn't fix the alternator, but a conscientious professional driver aware of the problem could have kept the car running. So, my friend, it's your fault, not the car's! The money stays with us!

Gamification 10/10

Paragraph	Only A OR B	Both A AND B
88 Ways of dressing	☐ 0 points	☐ 1 point
89 Discomforts and suffering	☐ 0 points	☐ 1 point
90 Social network - II	☐ 0 points	☐ 1 point
91 My son-in-law	☐ 0 points	☐ 1 point
92 Kindness and public transportation - I	☐ 0 points	☐ 1 point
93 Kindness and public transportation - II	☐ 0 points	☐ 1 point
94 Infants and weaning	☐ 0 points	☐ 1 point
95 Peace and war	☐ 0 points	☐ 1 point
96 Peace and revenge	☐ 0 points	☐ 1 point
97 Bullying and cyberbullying	☐ 0 points	☐ 1 point
98 Social network - III	☐ 0 points	☐ 1 point
99 Women judging women	☐ 0 points	☐ 1 point
100 Mediocrity on the track	☐ 0 points	☐ 1 point
TOTAL		

Bonus

101 The table at the restaurant

Viliberto, 9:10 PM on any given day

I love having lunch or dinner at a restaurant... not every day, of course, as that wouldn't be economically sustainable, but I find it delightful to go there with family or friends, or even, during the week, with clients and suppliers from my company. And it's always lovely to experience the ceremony of choosing: reading reviews to decide whether to visit a new place never tried before or to go to the usual, reliable, favorite restaurant! Once seated at my table, I find invaluable the pleasure of... browsing the menu. Sometimes this operation ends with the epiphanic discovery of a new, excellent dish that meets all the expectations, other times, instead, it results in... the wreck of all hopes! But this too is part of the ceremony! You often meet acquaintances there and, just like with the menu, sometimes you get lucky, other times... less so. You might meet acquaintances who love privacy, taking a break from their hectic lives to enjoy a moment of relaxation. This type of person, to which I proudly belong, greets you cordially but quickly, not keen on starting long conversations or opening chapters that are then hard to close. At most, they quickly ask you how you are, smiling, and then return to their place, to their comfort zone. But you can also meet that acquaintance who asks you to join him (!!!) and, even before you've had the chance to decline, he's already calling the waiter to add chairs. I hate that! At that point, to stop him, you turn directly to the waiter and say, with a clenched jaw, that you appreciate the friend's invitation, but you prefer to stay at your table. And then there are the lovely friends... the ones you love meeting because they are discreet people you truly care about and who genuinely care about you. But even this has its limits. It has often happened to me to meet dear friends with their families. But when fate makes their table close to yours not once, not twice, but many times and on many consecutive days, it's not necessarily a pleasant experience. This recently happened with a family of friends... The first encounter was fantastic, I was really happy. By the third encounter, I was starting to get nervous. Yes, because in the end, even if meeting them is enjoyable, you're no longer free to talk about everything, like when there are strangers instead (who, rest assured, couldn't care less about you). You can't discuss sensitive topics, talk about, say, work issues or problems your children are facing. You have to lower your voice and maintain a low profile because every 10 minutes at least, there's some cross-over between the tables. A joke shouted too loudly, one table getting involved in the dynamics of the other, an embarrassing glance. In short, I love these friends, but since we've been meeting so frequently, I no longer enjoy the restaurant moment as I used to. When I see them there again, always there, I think to myself... really? Again? I can't take it anymore... Sooner or later, I'll decide to change restaurants. But it's absurd to be forced into this! A doubt arises... what if the headwaiter, seeing the obvious mutual affection and emotional bond between us, had decided on his own to deliberately place us next to each other? It must be so, it can't just be a statistical anomaly. Come on! Even once, by the law of large numbers, their table should have been elsewhere! I'll talk to the waiter and, if it really turns out to be his initiative, I would thank him without making him feel awkward, but kindly ask him to position us a bit farther from my friends, explaining that although there's a strong friendship, we would occasionally like to enjoy a moment of true privacy to converse freely among ourselves. And if on that occasion I discover it wasn't the waiter's initiative, but my friends', not necessarily to be near us, but maybe because they like a particular table, I would ask to be placed a bit farther away. Today, instead of making a phone reservation, I'll stop by the restaurant in person to resolve the matter and rid myself of this embarrassment once and for all!

Viliberto, 9:10 PM on the same day...

I am indignant... more than that, indignant and angry, angry and disgusted! As expected, today, after work, here I am stopping by the restaurant The Diabetic Cat to talk with the headwaiter, who, recognizing me immediately, greets me warmly since I am – surely – one of his best customers. I tell him about the last seven times our table was placed next to that of my friends. I reassure him by saying that there is no issue with the restaurant, we would simply prefer to be a bit distant from them so as not to spend those two hours in discomfort, speaking in low voices. He smiles, seems to understand my request, and casually tells me that the arrangement has always been purely coincidental, especially since the room isn't that big. He explains, with an even broader smile, that there will be no problem accommodating both of us from now on by placing us at slightly less adjacent tables. I notice with curiosity the use of the term "both," but before probing further, I prefer to ask him why he is smiling. He replies that just today, a few minutes before my arrival, my friend also stopped by for the... same reasons, privacy and embarrassment, and asked him to place their table at a certain distance from ours from now on.

[... a long, very long pause of silence and dismay]

I must have misunderstood.

[… more silence]

But what is this idiot saying?

[silence, silence, silence]

Slowly, I recover from the initial shock. The first sensation I experience is a shiver running down my spine. Did I hear correctly? No, come on, I must have misunderstood the story from this moronic restaurateur in front of me. I ask the mediocre individual to explain everything again, and he confirms it. The second thing I think about is that I might have even run the risk of encountering my friend while he was here for this incredibly rude request! This triggers something even stronger and deeper within me, a shiver like... the need to pee. Slowly, the meaning of the words from the misfit speaking to me becomes clear. And gradually, the affront resulting from it starts to burn, damaging my inner mechanisms, unleashing my thoughts until they explode into an almost uncontrollable rage, which I manage to contain at the last moment by looking at the smiling face of the inept and foolish headwaiter who almost mocks me and, without a single word, is practically saying to me: 'You ask me to move your table to stay away from someone who, according to you, values your presence so much that they aren't disturbed by it at all, in fact... and who, above all – you say – doesn't mind the invasion of privacy... when, in reality, that someone wants to stay away from you and hates the situation as much as you do'. Okay. I don't want to kill the slightly unlikable headwaiter because I understand perfectly that I'm cornered in the ring. Let's summarize the situation. My friend asked this little character in front of me to ensure that from now on he gets a table far from mine. And he came here specifically to make this request. I can't believe it. How dare he? What is he insinuating? Is our company of little value? At those times, we never disturb him, we are always reluctant to start conversations. So does even our mere presence disturb him? How the hell does this jerk have the audacity? We barely notice his presence when we're here; in fact, I'd say even more, he's completely transparent to our eyes. We always maintain exemplary behavior at those times. I am truly disgusted. It's absurd. I would like to call him out and tell him off, and if I don't, it's only because I would then have to avoid this restaurant, my favorite, forever. But then... how can you interrupt your workday just to come here to ask this thing from the idiotic misfit in front of me? Was it so damn important to do so? I was at least nearby, and this place is almost on the way; I passed by after work and came in because this crude human being who is the headwaiter has always been more than just an acquaintance, at least until now. I came in because it seemed like such a small, almost insignificant request that would improve our evenings here a bit. And instead, my – now ex – friend does what? Works on the other side of the city, with very different hours, and stops by here to ask to distance us from him! I am stunned, dumbfounded. And, ironically, I can't even, I shouldn't, I don't want to confront him! Fine. Understood. Angrily, I tell the headwaiter of this godforsaken restaurant, which resembles a gas station in the desert, that it's okay with me. By moving the tables, he'll satisfy two of his customers instead of one. I leave with a huge rage inside me, but so huge...

252

Conclusions

Writing a book is easy. The hard part is convincing the world that it is worth reading.

J.K. Rowling

Author's Notes

We are all Jekyll... we are all Hyde. There is no condemnation in this statement, no tribunal, only a sincere self-assessment. The goal of this book, in fact, is not to teach the reader to avoid cognitive dissonance, but simply to accompany them in a process of recognizing the... *dissonant self.*

When, immersed in the crowd, I am a fundamental part of it, when I am an atomic element of a mass made up of people-atoms, but at the same time I claim to detest that very mass by distancing myself in the act of my scornful judgment, blaming other individual-atoms like myself and imagining myself as different from them, in those moments I might stubbornly stick to my positions and continue to harbor unfounded hatred, or alternatively, I could *grant my anger a moment of respite* and use it to understand the obvious and apparent dissonance inherent in my evaluation. To waste words explaining it further would nullify this book, whose sole objective, as already stated, is to *ignite*, where lacking, a new sensitivity capable of making that dissonance evident.

Forgive the mediocrity of this writing. For me, it is a debut work and for that reason, I will be proud of it regardless. It will certainly reflect the artistic immaturity of a self-styled writer, but if it is universally accepted that a book can emerge from a strong creative impulse, like any other work of art, the genesis of this text falls precisely into this case. Dreaming it, writing it, revising it, and tending to all its aspects have given me immense emotions that I will surely want to experience again, sooner or later. I hope it pleases someone, but if not, I will have still derived great joy from it.

Thank you all in any case!

Afterword *by Anonymous*

One, No One, and One Hundred Thousand... Human bodies are constantly transforming, taking on different forms depending on the observer's point of view. But what happens when the observer is me? How does my body appear to my own eyes?

I find myself sitting at a cozy café, sipping my usual espresso, while watching the main street of my small town, crossed by more or less familiar faces. Some I know well, others only superficially, though I know their entire history, while others are friends of a lifetime.

The barista greets me with a smile as I enter, and after the usual pleasantries, prepares my coffee. The lady who lives across from the café warmly greets me, inquiring about my well-being and that of my loved ones. I respond with a smile, reassuring her that everything is going well. Then an old friend arrives, and we stop to chat, sharing the latest news while enjoying our coffee.

I am the regular customer for breakfast, a kind and smiling woman. I am the daughter of a longtime friend, a cheerful, accomplished person, always present when a smile or kind word is needed. I am a lifelong friend, constant in support, ready to listen and share joys and sorrows, to celebrate successes and comfort in defeats.

Does the image I project of myself, sitting at the table with a smile, truly reflect my real identity, or is it simply the result of behaviors I adopt to match the image I want to convey?

How close are my Real Self and my Ideal Self?

Is my self-perception based on interactions with others, or is it an intrinsic aspect, with others acting only as a mirror to reflect it? How close are my Real Self and my Social Self?

I watch the street, lost in my thoughts, and there she is. Perhaps an ex-friend, Gilda. I haven't seen her for at least a year, and the last time I called her, she wasn't feeling well. Since then, I haven't been able to reach her; I've been very busy and she was always unavailable.

Yes, that's how it went. She was going through a tough time, that's true… we used to hang out with friends, and she wanted to be alone. One day she even asked me to leave her alone... so what? What could I do? I couldn't be intrusive or insistent; at that moment she needed to process her sadness alone. Calling her and offering support would have been annoying and intrusive. Better to wait until the storm passed and we could laugh and joke again in the open air, at the sea and in the wind.

But then why do I feel so uncomfortable as she approaches?

She looks at me from afar, passes by, and chats with the café owner, exchanging jokes and laughs. I remain seated, not getting up, waiting for her to leave while pretending to send messages on my phone.

Why did she pretend not to see me? But more importantly… why did I pretend not to see her?

I think back to what happened with her and remember the exact moment I decided not to contact her again; she was really rude. I rang her doorbell after a day's work and found her in pajamas eating chips on the couch. She felt sad and didn't want to do anything, not even chat. I shared some work problems, and she seemed completely uninterested. So I left. She didn't even see me to the door; she didn't get up from the couch, just waved a melancholic goodbye.

Shortly after, in the busiest café in town, a mutual friend, Sara, arrives. Earlier, Sara and Gilda had met a few meters from the café and exchanged warm greetings, a few jokes, and then went their ways.

Sara enters the café, sees me sitting alone, and comes over, smiling, sitting down to chat about this and that. Then she talks about Gilda, saying she is really happy to see her happy again, and that she's been seeing a new partner and has been revived for the past few months.

The fact that she's updating me on Gilda's life means she's aware of our estrangement. So I decide to share my experience with her, hoping to make her understand that it wasn't my choice not to see Gilda anymore. Perhaps I'm trying to convince myself?

I repeat to her what my mind had just gone over, and she, though nodding, reminds me that Gilda had called and contacted me several times in the months following that incident. She wasn't well and knew she had been unfriendly, but I hadn't replied.

My mind retrieves those memories. Me looking at the phone and seeing Gilda's name on the screen, me sighing and thinking… no, what a hassle, pretending I missed the call. Me not reading the message… after all, who reads texts anymore?

This is confirmation bias… a cognitive prejudice where we favor information that confirms our preexisting beliefs or hypotheses, while disregarding or ignoring evidence that contradicts our starting ideas. Our minds distort information, seeking data that supports our thesis and downplaying contrary information. If we encounter incongruent information, we dismiss it or use it to support and reinforce our ideas.

I explain to Sara that I probably didn't respond because I was contacted during work hours, and Gilda's intention was to distance herself, evidenced by her calls at inconvenient times or the now outdated texts. Additionally, I had been going through a rough patch; otherwise, I would have certainly called her back, but I wasn't doing well myself.

Given my nature, I would hardly abandon a friend in difficulty.

Sara doesn't seem very convinced, but she nods… after all, she doesn't really care about my friendship with Gilda; it was just a chat. She drinks her coffee and says goodbye.

I remain there at the table, a half-hour breakfast that made me revisit the mechanisms of a lifetime.

When I am good, kind, available, pleasant, and wonderful… well, what can I do… it's my character… but when I am calculating, cruel, lacking empathy, individualistic… well, what can I do… I'm going through a rough patch.

I often wonder if the narrative we construct about ourselves traps us in a role we desire but that doesn't truly belong to us or if, conversely, it limits us in a role we don't desire but which doesn't represent us. Perhaps it's just a way to continuously justify ourselves for failures and choices we consider wrong and for which we don't want to take responsibility.

Frequently, I talk to friends who attribute their work failures to their impulsive character, their honesty, their direct way of always saying what they think. Partly, they might be right: perhaps an impulsive reaction led to certain consequences on specific occasions. This self-narrative leads those who truly know them, as well as those who don't, to view them as straightforward individuals, often labeled as "annoying" because they leave nothing to chance.

But how often have they truly behaved so directly? Perhaps once or twice in a lifetime. Yet, by repeating it and due to human acquiescence – that which makes you nod without contesting anything when talking to people and leads you to reinforce their beliefs simply because you don't really care about what they say – often timid individuals end up feeling like lions.

I wonder if the course of events in our lives is the result of a self-fulfilling prophecy, whether positive or negative. Is it possible that everything that happens to us is influenced by a hidden expectation, by a deep-seated belief that silently guides our steps? When I look in the mirror, I wonder if I am real or just a fictitious figure, a projection of my thoughts and beliefs. Are we real? Are we fictitious? And for whom are we?

Perhaps our reality is different depending on the eyes that observe us. To some, we might be solid and tangible, while to others, we might be fleeting shadows, ephemeral images.

Perhaps we are both things simultaneously: real and fictitious, a duality that coexists without conflict. Our essence might be a living paradox, an intertwining of truths and illusions that dance together. And in this dance, the self-fulfilling prophecy might be the invisible thread that weaves our destiny, a destiny that eludes us yet defines us, a destiny that makes us who we are, for better or worse.

We desperately try to maintain the positive idea we have of ourselves, attempting to eliminate emotions we consider bad or wrong. And if we experience negative feelings, in order to assert that they don't belong to us, we blame others, shifting the flaws and criticisms directed at us or that dance in the deepest part of ourselves onto them.

At that point, we manage to transform our attitudes into their attitudes, and by judging them, we become superior and distant. But why does this happen? Why can't we be consistent with our ideas and beliefs?

Blind Spot... the Blind Spot... let's talk about those black spots that prevent us from clearly seeing our behaviors.

The interpretation of our actions is subjective, it tells our story, our successes, our failures, traumas, and tenderness, helping us maintain that necessary balance that allows us to be serene, to stay in the comfort zone. In our continuous, desperate search for consonance, we distance ourselves from those who are different from us and seek those who resemble us, who think like us, because we don't like disagreement. And if something is dissonant, we redefine ourselves to make it consonant.

The comfort zone is that feeling of familiarity and security that often keeps us trapped in a gray zone of dissatisfaction and tranquility. Often it is a terrible and treacherous zone, but we know it and can control it. And even when it is far scarier than uncertainty, we tend to choose it because we know its map. How important is the discomfort we feel in our lives? How capable is it of stimulating our changes? But why and for what should we want and need to change?

We spend our lives waiting for a magical moment, as if at some point something extraordinary should happen to reward us for all the efforts made and imagined. In the meantime, we try to adapt to life and the world, sometimes sacrificing our present happiness for future happiness. We imagine changing, improving ourselves, convinced that at some point all the pieces of the puzzle will fit together perfectly, and we will finally be able to enjoy it all. But we don't even know what this entails, we don't know what could truly make us happy.

Our daily lives are populated by ghost lives that could have made us more satisfied, more fulfilled. They are full of unburied skeletons, untraveled paths, unimagined joys, unaddressed unhappiness. Perhaps none of us truly change because perhaps none of us is ever something definitive; we pursue an integrity that doesn't exist.

What if we were all simultaneously the same and different at every moment? What if we were merely the personal and social projection of external conditions? What if I were not truly myself, the one I believe I am, but rather you (you, the reader) and everyone else? We are different with every person we meet and for every person we meet, but we need to always feel the same to ourselves. Probably, true wisdom lies in accepting uncertainty and living authentically each moment, aware that our true self is in constant evolution and that the search for ourselves is an endless journey.

Paradoxically, the only consistency we possess is our constant inconsistency.

The author of this wonderful afterword has requested to remain anonymous. I thank her from the bottom of my heart for her invaluable contribution.

Gamification: check your score!

Our game ends here. By recording the scores from each chapter in the score column, you'll get an approximate percentage of the impact of cognitive dissonance in your life. This is clearly a rough, unreliable assessment, but it's unlikely that the total will be zero. It will be interesting to know how often phenomena like those described occur in your daily life.

	Title	Score
	Methodological approach	
Chapter 1	In the car	
Chapter 2	Religion and devotion	
Chapter 3	Ecology	
Chapter 4	World of work	
Chapter 5	State, politics, services	
Chapter 6	Society	
Chapter 7	Love and sexuality	
Chapter 8	Peoples and culture	
Chapter 9	Your neighbor	
TOTAL		

Thank you for playing, for your honesty, but most of all, thank you for revealing here, without too much hesitation, the many and contrasting versions of yourself that each of us displays every day!

Acknowledgements

The first and biggest thanks goes to my life partner, wife, and mother of my children, Chiara, an irreplaceable source of motivation and testing ground for me. I am the perfect example of someone who constantly and in the worst way experiences bipolar ethics, often absolving myself while accusing others even more frequently. The witness to this recurring alternation is she, Chiara, who, rather than being a merciless judge, wants to lovingly help me understand that none of us is free from similar behaviors. When she hears me judging someone harshly and realizes that I have behaved the same way at another time, she gently points it out to me. This, immediately, triggers in me a painful itch that gradually becomes annoyance, amplifying the existing discomfort stemming from the dissonance itself. But it also leads me, today more than before, to reflect deeply on the issue. Discovering oneself to be inconsistent, a partial judge, an unfair arbiter, presents two paths: on one hand, one can reject the accusations, labeling them as insinuations; on the other, through constant effort, recognize the inconsistency, the dissonance, the bipolarity, and transform this suffering into a creative moment. And I hope this has made me, even if only imperceptibly for now, better. Thank you, Chiara, because none of this would have been possible without you.

The second thanks goes to my friends and former colleagues Roberto Covitti and Renata Isaia who, for almost two years, every Friday, in front of an excellent traditional or Neapolitan pizza, would ask me regularly about the progress of the text, giving me suggestions, providing another point of view, always welcome and valuable. Thank you, Roberto, for your constant interest and your suggestions. Thank you, Renata, for your essential contribution to the design and realization of the cover and for your suggestions on the layout. You gave me an incredible boost not to give up even when fatigue and the desire to sleep a bit longer in the morning, rather than writing, were about to take over. Thank you, the music inside you becomes a symphony outside.

Thanks also to my dear friend and colleague, Fabio Testini, who often joins our Friday lunches, always giving his valuable opinion on how to do things in the best way.

The third thanks goes to a friend. Not just any friend, the only one, the most important, Mariangela Palma. No amount of wisdom or treatises can describe and explain the strong bond we have experienced since childhood. Thank you, Mariangela, for not giving suggestions for this project, for not criticizing, judging, underestimating, or ridiculing me. You simply listened, as you always do, reacting with great enthusiasm to the updates I communicated to you every week, encouraging me. This energy helped me maintain the healthy and crucial – for me – illusion that I could really make it.

I also want to thank three pillars of my life. Essential and irreplaceable friends. By a brilliant and wonderful sliding doors coincidence, we have been accomplices since 1986. Always present, always close. Us, still together, with our irreplaceable humorous mutual derision, us in front of many beers, still talking about ourselves, music, dramas, medicine, psychology, and then immediately after about crazy paradoxes, improbable nonsense, and comic epics that still, as 40 years ago, make us laugh until we cry, pajamas included. A sincere thank you to you too for always listening with interest to my updates about this project. Thank you, legendary Marco Torres, Claudio Cantinieri, Donato Vinci. Thank you, Whirling Cocks!

Thanks to the friends who received this writing with curiosity. Perhaps no one will read it, but I am relatively indifferent to that. I have achieved my goal... writing is a unique experience.

Finally, a posthumous thank you to the unforgettable Brunella Soldani, professor of History and Philosophy, and Bruno Di Rienzo, professor of Italian and Latin, unforgettable teachers during my wonderful and crucial (six) years (1984-1989) of high school, which began and ended in via Celso Ulpiani at the dilapidated but beloved Liceo Scientifico Statale Enrico Fermi in Bari, section B.

Thank you certainly for the legendary lessons and examinations, but especially for having justly failed me in the third year. The good you did for me is enormous. I had experienced those first three years very poorly. I asked to change sections, but fortunately, the headmaster denied the request. Then a certain Claudio, my curious future classmate, evidently free from prejudices about failures, expressed to a mutual friend the desire to meet the new repeating colleague. The rest is history. I found myself magically in the best class and with the best friends in the world. And with them, I overcame, to use terms from mathematical analysis, a cusp in my life, with a negative left derivative and a positive right derivative. That failure is perhaps the most useful event that has ever happened to me. It transformed my life and gave me eternal friendships. I owe almost everything I am today to that event.

Dear professors, I had embarked on a direction without a future, and you put me back on track. If this book exists, it is thanks to the seed you planted in those crazy and incredible years. I will never forget you.

May the earth be light upon you.

Roberto De Nicolò

266

Plato: The Allegory of the Cave

[*omitted*] **Socrates**: And now, let me show in a figure how far our nature is enlightened or unenlightened: — Behold! human beings living in a underground den, which has a mouth open towards the light and reaching all along the den; here they have been from their childhood, and have their legs and necks chained so that they cannot move, and can only see before them, being prevented by the chains from turning round their heads. Above and behind them a fire is blazing at a distance, and between the fire and the prisoners there is a raised way; and you will see, if you look, a low wall built along the way, like the screen which marionette players have in front of them, over which they show the puppets. **Glaucon:** I see.

Socrates: And do you see men passing along the wall carrying all sorts of vessels, and statues and figures of animals made of wood and stone and various materials, which appear over the wall? Some of them are talking, others silent. **Glaucon:** You have shown me a strange image, and they are strange prisoners. **Socrates:** Like ourselves; and they see only their own shadows, or the shadows of one another, which the fire throws on the opposite wall of the cave? **Glaucon:** True; how could they see anything but the shadows if they were never allowed to move their heads? **Socrates:** And of the objects which are being carried in like manner they would only see the shadows? **Glaucon:** Yes. **Socrates:** And if they were able to converse with one another, would they not suppose that they were naming what was actually before them? **Glaucon:** Very true. **Socrates:** And suppose further that the prison had an echo which came from the other side, would they not be sure to fancy when one of the passers-by spoke that the voice which they heard came from the passing shadow? **Glaucon:** No question. **Socrates:** To them the truth would be literally nothing but the shadows of the images. **Glaucon:** That is certain.

Socrates: And now look again, and see what will naturally follow if the prisoners are released and disabused of their error. At first, when any of them is liberated and compelled suddenly to stand up and turn his neck round and walk and look towards the light, he will suffer sharp pains; the glare will distress him, and he will be unable to see the realities of which in his former state he had seen the shadows; and then conceive some one saying to him, that what he saw before was an illusion, but that now, when he is approaching nearer to being and his eye is turned towards more real existence, he has a clearer vision, — what will be his reply? And you may further imagine that his instructor is pointing to the objects as they pass and requiring him to name them, — will he not be perplexed? Will he not fancy that the shadows which he formerly saw are truer than the objects which are now shown to him? **Glaucon:** Far truer.

Socrates: And if he is compelled to look straight at the light, will he not have a pain in his eyes which will make him turn away to take and take in the objects of vision which he can see, and which he will conceive to be in reality clearer than the things which are now being shown to him? **Glaucon:** True. **Socrates:** And suppose once more, that he is reluctantly dragged up a steep and rugged ascent, and held fast until he's forced into the presence of the sun himself, is he not likely to be pained and irritated? When he approaches the light his eyes will be dazzled, and he will not be able to see anything at all of what are now called realities. **Glaucon:** Not all in a moment. **Socrates:** He will require to grow accustomed to the sight of the upper world. And first he will see the shadows best, next the reflections of men and other objects in the water, and then the objects themselves; then he will gaze upon the light of the moon and the stars and the spangled heaven; and he will see the sky and the stars by night better than the sun or the light of the sun by day? **Glaucon:** Certainly.

Socrates: Last of he will be able to see the sun, and not mere reflections of him in the water, but he will see him in his own proper place, and not in another; and he will contemplate him as he is. **Glaucon:** Certainly. **Socrates:** He will then proceed to argue that this is he who gives the season and the years, and is the guardian of all that is in the visible world, and in a certain way the cause of all things which he and his fellows have been accustomed to behold? **Glaucon:** Clearly, he would first see the sun and then reason about him. **Socrates:** And when he remembered his old habitation, and the wisdom of the den and his fellow-prisoners, do you not suppose that he would felicitate himself on the change, and pity them? **Glaucon:** Certainly, he would. **Socrates:** And if they were in the habit of conferring honours among themselves on those who were quickest to observe the passing shadows and to remark which of them went before, and which followed after, and which were together; and who were therefore best able to draw conclusions as to the future, do you think that he would care for such honours and glories, or envy the possessors of them? Would he not say with Homer, Better to be the poor servant of a poor master, and to endure anything, rather than think as they do and live after their manner? **Glaucon:** Yes, I think that he would rather suffer anything than entertain these false notions and live in this miserable manner. **Socrates:** Imagine once more, such an one coming suddenly out of the sun to be replaced in his old situation; would he not be certain to have his eyes full of darkness? **Glaucon:** To be sure. **Socrates:** And if there were a contest, and he had to compete in measuring the shadows with the prisoners who had never moved out of the den, while his sight was still weak, and before his eyes had become steady (and the time which would be needed to acquire this new habit of sight might be very considerable) would he not be ridiculous? Men would say of him that up he went and down he came without his eyes; and that it was better not even to think of ascending; and if any one tried to loose another and lead him up to the light, let them only catch the offender, and they would put him to death. **Glaucon:** No question.

Socrates: This entire allegory, you may now append, dear Glaucon, to the previous argument; the prison-house is the world of sight, the light of the fire is the sun, and you will not misapprehend me if you interpret the journey upwards to be the ascent of the soul into the intellectual world according to my poor belief, which, at your desire, I have expressed whether rightly or wrongly God knows. But, whether true or false, my opinion is that in the world of knowledge the idea of good appears last of all, and is seen only with an effort; and, when seen, is also inferred to be the universal author of all things beautiful and right, parent of light and of the lord of light in this visible world, and the immediate source of reason and truth in the intellectual; and that this is the power upon which he who would act rationally, either in public or private life, must have his eye fixed. [*omitted*]

("Allegory of the Cave" from The Republic by Plato (380 B.C.) is in the public domain.

BIPOLAR ETHICS

A book by **Roberto De Nicolò** aka *rodenic*

Cover design by **Renata Isaia** aka *Reis*

Cover image **Generative AI / Shutterstock**

Afterword by **Anonymous**

Available also in: **Italian language** – by **rodenic**

Coming soon also in: **Audiobook** – narrated by **rodenic**

This book was entirely written using:

LibreOffice - www.libreoffice.org

For information and updates:

rodenic@gmail.com

First edition

ISBN: 9798343246841

Publisher: Independently published

October 2024